DEFINE Wh
WANT

1) Passionate - for Gr
for PEOPLE

2) Fun -

3) Forward momentum.

4) Place I WANNA Be AT!

    A. IF our church is
    Not a place I want
    to go or be apart
    or - well, make
    change!

5) Friendly -

6) Real
7) Honest
8) Authentic.
9) Relationships

The Up the Middle Church
...playing the game of ministry one yard at a time...

Matt Keller

authorHOUSE®

AuthorHouse™
1663 Liberty Drive, Suite 200
Bloomington, IN 47403
www.authorhouse.com
Phone: 1-800-839-8640

First published by AuthorHouse 12/11/2008

ISBN: 978-1-4389-3574-4 (sc)
ISBN: 978-1-4389-3573-7 (hc)

Printed in the United States of America
Bloomington, Indiana

This book is printed on acid-free paper.

Cover Design by Ariel Morejon

www.UptheMiddle.com

Praise for

The Up-the-Middle Church

"Matt Keller represents a phenomenal young voice in the church world today. I interact with some of the top leaders in the country today and Matt is at the top of that list! He gets it. Matt is someone I trust and respect as a leading voice in the future growth of the church and Christianity as a whole."

- CHAD JOHNSON, The Catalyst Conference

"*The Up the Middle Church* is a helpful resource for the rest of us-- church planters and leaders of small churches. The principles in this book have the ability to transform churches and help them breakthrough to the next level. In real world ministry, the church does not explode to thousands the first year. It is hard work and can be a challenge. *The Up the Middle Church* will be a refreshment to everyone living in an up-the-middle real world church."

- ED STETZER, author, *Lost and Found: The Younger Unchurched and Churches that Reach Them*

"Matt Keller captures the essence of church planting and reminds us that time and tenacity are required to move the ball down the field. Matt is part of a great organization called ARC that plants scores of vibrant, growing churches each year."

- JOHN C. MAXWELL, Founder INJOY Stewardship Services & EQUIP

"*The Up the Middle Church* is a must read for pastors who feel stuck in the church growth process. In his entertaining and readable style, Matt Keller offers both practical nuts and bolts as well as catalytic big ideas that will help to transform your church from average to extraordinary."

- JOHN BOLIN, Author & Creative Director for the Association of Related Churches

"When I read *The Up The Middle Church*, I exclaimed, "Finally, a guy is talking about the things I need to hear!" We needed practical information that dealt with real-life church issues. Matt writes from the trenches for those in the trenches."

- AARON MANERS, Lead Pastor, Canvas Church, Jacksonville, FL

"*The Up the Middle Church* is for all those leaders who have a divine vision and are waiting to see it come to fruition. In our times of discouragement Keller's principles have taught us to stop comparing ourselves with the ministries we read about and to be secure in the vision God has given us."

- JOSHUA GAGNON, Lead Pastor, NLC.tv

"*The Up The Middle Church* is a must read for all pastors today. Too many pastors nowadays feel alone and wonder if they're making a difference. Matt does a great job of speaking to their heart by giving them both insight and the practical help they need to take their church to a place of impacting their community for Christ."

- RANDY BEZET, Lead Pastor, Bayside Community Church, Bradenton, FL

"Matt and Sarah are passionate about the success of churches. Through their experience expressed in the pages of *The Up the Middle Church*, they give real help for those of us in the trenches. This book is a must-read for all church leaders and their friends."

- Barry Rice, Lead Pastor, Greater Orlando Church, Orlando,FL

"This is more than a church planting book. This is a book about how to lead a new church plant to significant growth and impact. Matt offers a rare and needed perspective from the playing field. A must read for anyone who dares to go for it on fourth and long."

- DAVID PUTNAM, Founder of *churchplanters.com* & co-author of *Breaking the Discipleship Code*

The Up-the-Middle Church
Published by Up-the-Middle Resources

To Sarah,
Can you believe we get to do this?
We are truly living the dream, and there is no one
else I would rather be living this dream with.
You still light up my room!

I love you,
Matt

Contents

Foreword

I really like the premise of this book. I've often described the church I lead, Seacoast Church, as the slowest growing mega church in America. We opened with 340 people the first Sunday and didn't reach that number again in average attendance for five years.

I remember hearing about churches that immediately rocketed into the stratosphere and immediately becoming discouraged at our lack of progress. *"What was wrong with us?"* I questioned my call, our strategy, and on many occasions wanted to give up and do something else.

I wish Matt Keller would have written this book back then. I like this guy. He's one of us...not flashy or all that hip. Just determined and committed to doing the little things right. He encourages us that just because we don't connect with the long bomb right away, God still has a plan for us.

I'm reminded of Galatians 6:9 - *"Let us not become weary in doing good, for at the proper time we will reap a harvest if we do not give up."*

That is Matt's story, it is my story, and it could be yours also. Keep running it up-the-middle and who knows, God just might use your church to do things in your city that will surprise everyone...maybe even you.

D I Believe
9/2015

Greg Surratt

Seacoast Church,
Charleston, SC

There's a New Normal in the Church World!

"Everybody loves a long-bomb... unfortunately, few of us get to experience one!"

I t's fourth down and long. Time is running out. The game is on the line. The hush of the crowd is deafening, and everyone is on the edge of their seats. The quarterback takes the snap, feels the blitz breaking through his offensive line and looks down field for an open receiver. He lets the football fly. It lands perfectly between the two defenders surrounding his receiver. And somehow, by some amazing miracle, the receiver catches it and takes off in a dead sprint for the goal line.

The crowd jumps to their feet as they realize their team has won! As the receiver crosses the goal line and scores the winning touchdown, thousands of fans scream with all their might in amazement and jubilation. The story of this victory will be retold hundreds of times around water coolers! Cameras capture the moment for the highlight reels! This is truly one for the ages! Everyone loves a long-bomb!

Long-Bombs in the Church World

We love to hear the stories of churches that start in faith, and within a few short months are living the long-bomb. We love to hear of thousands in weekend attendance in the first year. We dream of what it would be like to be apart of something God visits that way. We all dream of being the long-bomb!

We love to watch those churches, study their tactics, and learn from them. We want to hear what they did, how they did it, and when they did it. We long to grab a hold of that little nugget that will let *us* become like *them*. Something about the overnight success story inspires us to want to do what they did. We long for our church to look like theirs. We aspire to walk in their footsteps, and experience what they experienced.

We look to them for inspiration, direction, and leadership. And we should. The success stories of many of the great churches of our day serve as models and examples of what God is capable of doing through willing vessels.

One such story is Church of the Highlands in Birmingham, AL, pastored by my friend Chris Hodges. In just a few short years, Highlands has become one of the premiere churches in America and Chris's voice influences thousands of leaders across the nation, including mine. I absolutely admire Chris and the Highlands team for what God has accomplished through them. They are truly a long-bomb story.

But their story is not my story. And the reality for most pastors today is that their story doesn't look like the long-bomb, so many of us feel pressure to live up to the long-bomb story. Consequently, many of us become disillusioned and discouraged. When our story doesn't look like the overnight success, we see no other option but to feel discouraged. If we're not careful, we can be tempted to believe our destiny is mediocrity, and that type of mindset can lead to a defeated leader leading a defeated church.

More Than One Play in the Playbook

What if it doesn't have to be this way? What if there is more than one way to win? What if the long-bomb isn't the only play God is using today? What if God's strategy to impact the nations centers on more than just the long-bomb churches? What if there's hope for the rest of us? After all, we know the game is not won or lost by the long-bomb play alone.

Think of the NFL. What if every team only used the long-bomb as their offensive strategy? It wouldn't take long before the defense would know exactly how to stop them week in and week out. NFL teams know that a more comprehensive offensive strategy is necessary if they're going to build a winning franchise. And the same thing is true in the Kingdom of God. God needs a strategy that includes both long-bomb churches and up-the-middle churches if we're going to accomplish the fulfillment of the great commission.

A New Normal in the Church World

I believe there is a new "normal" emerging in the church world today. That new normal is the up-the-middle church. I used to wish our story was a long-bomb, but not anymore. Our story is an up-the-middle story. We have lived the reality of building a church one yard at a time. We know what it means to pastor four people, forty-four people, 444 people, and 744 people.

Along the way we've had our share of fumbles, punts, and roughing-the-passer calls. But I wouldn't trade the lessons we've learned and the yards we've gained for any other church growth story on the planet. What began as four people in a coffee shop with a lot of vision and zero clue has grown into a church that is making an impact on our region of the country and around the world. We are an up-the-middle church.

I want to grow slow & steady, focusing on adding people who live here w/ Jesus @ the center.

Chances are, you are too. Statistics tell us the vast majority of churches across the United States and around the world look more like up-the-middle churches, than long-bomb churches. It's apparent that a major part of God's offensive strategy includes the up-the-middle church.

Words of Wisdom from John Mellencamp

I think John Mellencamp said it best in his song, *Small Town* when he sang, *"I got nothin' against the big town…"* Let me say it again, we need the long-bomb churches. Several of my friends, like Chris Hodges and others, are long-bomb guys. I talk to them, watch them, and learn from them constantly. But doing church up-the-middle is a different reality than the long-bomb. Leading an up-the-middle church requires a different skill set.

This book is written for the up-the-middle church: The pastors and leaders doing church one yard at a time. In the pages of this book are the keys to running an up-the-middle offense. You'll hear the stories of big hits and tackles, as well as many first downs and touchdowns. If you're doing church up-the-middle, then read on. There's a Super Bowl ring with your name on it.

Who This Book Is For

This book is written for three groups of people. First are church planters. Those of us who dare to *go it alone* are truly a unique kind. If you're living the journey of church planting, then you've come across this book at exactly the right time. This book will serve you and your team well in the days ahead. Chances are you're already finding out that what you *expected* to experience and what you're *actually* experiencing are two different things.

The second group of people this book is for are pastors whose stories haven't been long-bombs either. Perhaps you find yourself in a church that isn't the long-bomb you dreamed it might be. If so, then take hope. This book will allow you to see that victory is possible! In the pages ahead, you'll see that by taking ground one yard at a time, you can win your Super Bowl no matter how deep in the end zone you may be today!

The third group of people this book is for are team members, staff, and leaders of up-the-middle churches. *The Up-the- Middle Church* will inspire you, challenge you, and encourage you! The lessons we've learned will give you a first-hand look at life inside your up-the-middle reality. I encourage you to study a chapter at a time together as a leadership team, and then spend time each week to discuss the perspectives you're learning. At the end of each chapter are a few *Questions for the Huddle* to help you get the conversation started. The principles in this book will help you gain real-time ministry experience that will position you and your church for long-term success for years to come.

If you fit any of those categories, welcome to the team. You hold in your hand a playbook of game-tested principles that will allow you to reach the goal line, one yard at a time! One thing is certain: You're not alone anymore! We're all in this together. Doing church up-the-middle, is truly a team sport, and I'm on your team. I've been where you are. I know what it is to be the little guy. And I want to share the lessons we've learned along the way one yard at a time.

The Overview of the Up-the-Middle Church

By being an up-the-middle church, we learned that our ministry strategy had to center around four major focal points. These focal points represent the four sections of this book.

Section 1 keys in on the <u>Practical Side</u> of the Up-the-Middle Church. Great teams know how to leverage their brand in the community, create a culture for long-term success, and use the power of marketing and buzz to generate momentum in their church.

Section 2 keys in on the <u>Process</u> of the Up-the-Middle Church. Four key elements must be in place in order to create wins for the up-the-middle church. Embracing an "everything matters" mindset, learning the power of voices, utilizing core process for assimilation, and optimizing facility for long-term gain are essentials for success in an up-the-middle reality.

Section 3 keys in on the <u>People</u> of the Up-the-middle Church. A team is only as strong as the individuals who make it up. Section 3 unpacks the ingredients up-the-middle churches must have in the leadership mix in order to be effective.

Finally, **Section 4** covers the <u>Personal Side</u> of the Up-the-Middle Church. Staying healthy, establishing boundaries, knowing yourself, and redefining success are the final four objectives every up-the-middle pastor must put into practice if he intends to win the game of ministry one yard at a time.

In January 2002, we got in the game without the luxury of a step by step playbook. Over the past several years we've learned how to play. Victory can be achieved by doing church up-the-middle. *The Up-the-Middle Church* is the new normal in the church world. Long-bombs make highlight reels, but most of the game is actually played up-the-middle.

That's what this book is all about...

9/15

Our long Bombs are even/a/le
Dazzle hope some Jump + catch it but we'ie
to gwin it out --

Introduction

The Up-the-Middle Church

In the early days of our church, we adopted a saying that stuck with us, and we continue to use today. The phrase was, "up-the-middle." In fact, every time we thought God might be giving us a long-bomb, we realized it was, indeed, just another opportunity to go up-the-middle or at best a pass for a short yardage gain. Going up-the-middle has allowed us to learn so much along the way. It's been an incredible ride, to say the least.

It's easier to see now in hindsight the many lessons we would have completely missed had we been given the long-bomb we were praying for. I love seeing God's sovereignty in it all now. I would have loved for it to be easier, quicker, bigger, and faster *then*. But not now. Today, I'm thankful for every yard of our journey. I don't regret one ounce of sweat we've had to put into this. Seeing what Next Level Church has become today makes it all worth it!

The Early Days

When my wife and I relocated from Indiana in January of 2002 to start Next Level Church, we didn't have a clue what we were doing. We had done local church youth ministry for 4 years, and then spent three years traveling as National Youth Directors for a small fellowship of churches in the Midwest. But none of that could have prepared us for what we were about to experience.

7yrs ministry prior to planting

God! Tour yo!
9/15

Matt Keller

With $9,200, two college guys, an eighteen-month old son, and a 24 foot Ryder truck, we moved 1,300 miles away from the only home we had ever known to Fort Myers, FL. Both sets of parents helped us make the move from Indiana to Florida, and the first few days felt like we were on vacation, but then reality set in.

I remember the day we put our parents on the airplane to fly back to Indiana... without us. We felt so alone. So clueless. So grown up—all at the same time. Here we were living our dream and scared out of our minds.

We had heard somewhere that you needed a launch team, so in February we started a Bible study at a coffee shop in town. Week one... no one came. Week two... no one. It wasn't until week three that someone other than the four of us actually showed up. By Mother's Day (the absolute worst time to launch a church), we had ten adults and two kids. So we began. On May 12, 2002, Next Level Church was born—thirty-five people in a movie theater.

We spent the first four years in that movie theater, starting in the smallest theater. The memories of those days are still so vivid in my mind. No lights, a nasty old sound system, no drums. Just me, my guitar, and my wife singing harmony beside me. That was our worship band for the first year. It was primitive and hard. From thirty-five people on our launch Sunday to nineteen the next week, we finally settled in at a solid fifty through the summer months. We set our eyes on fall and geared up to move thirty feet to a slightly bigger theater in October, just to try and gain momentum.

Amazingly enough. it worked. By the time the church was five months old, we had a solid seventy people attending weekly, and enough income to allow me to quit my job in the jewelry store I had been working in for seven months. On our first Easter, we took a huge risk and sent out a 25,000 piece mailer that spiked our attendance and

8

allowed us to comfortably settle in just above the one hundred mark. I remember our 1ˢᵗ anniversary picnic having 102 in attendance. Those early days were hard… definitely up-the-middle.

By Christmas of 2003, the church was nineteen months old, and we were moving into the largest theater. I'll never forget the feeling I had when my wife told me we had 203 people there that Sunday. At the 2 year mark, we launched two services. (It was in the middle of two hurricanes. Did I mention I live in Florida?) It was the biggest fumble we had experienced yet. We spent thousands of dollars in advertising that literally blew away in the mailboxes of 40,000 homes across southwest Florida during the hurricanes. People weren't interested in finding a church; they were trying to get electricity!

All in all, we did 200 Sundays (exactly) in the Bell Tower Theaters. So many of the up-the-middle principles were learned in that movie theater. Movie theater church is a cool reality, but it's not without its challenges.

On Easter of 2006, with an average attendance of about 280, we moved to South Fort Myers High School, a brand new 40 million dollar facility. We really believed the move to the school would be a long-bomb. In fact, we fully expected to double within a few months of moving in. In the end, it was yet another up-the-middle short yardage gain.

We moved in April, and by June, our average attendance was about 330. However, in July and August, things dropped off numerically and financially, and I really thought that I had killed the church. With only 250 in total attendance (kids and adults) church felt more like a ghost town than the cool, hip movie theater church we had been just a few short months ago.

By October of 2006, momentum had returned, and we were off and running up-the-middle again. By our fifth Christmas, we had over

400 people in church. Our fifth anniversary service had 580 people in attendance. By implementing more and more of the up-the-middle principles we were learning, we were able to grow by another hundred people through the summer of 2007, and by our 6th Easter service, we saw our first jump above the 1,000 people mark. We continue to utilize the mobile reality of South Fort Myers High School and are excited about the long-term potential that a permanent facility has to offer us for our Sunday morning services.

In November of 2007, 5 ½ years after our launch, we moved into a 6,300 sq. ft. warehouse facility. This space has a 150 seat auditorium, Starbucks style café, as well as 3,000 sq. ft. of offices for our staff. This facility gives us options for so many of the medium-sized environments that we need to create now. Sunday mornings continue to happen in the high school, which is about a mile from our warehouse facility.

The vision of Next Level Church has always been a gigantic one. We see multi-site in our future. We have a huge heart to reproduce our DNA through church planting and world missions. Seeing a big vision has never been the difficult thing for us. In fact, reading the last few paragraphs of our story could make it sound easy. But as you'll hear throughout the pages of this book, what wasn't so easy was the dual reality we found ourselves living in the first few years.

The Dual Reality of the Up-the-Middle Concept

What a great privilege it is to pastor a church that has been small to medium-sized, and now is starting to feel big. Most days it's a joy and a headache, a blessing and a curse, a victory and a struggle. Yet, it's in that bi-polar feeling environment that we learned so many of the up-the-middle principles: Principles that have shaped Next Level Church into the church it has become today. We're not where we're going to be in a few years, but we're so much further than we were a few years ago.

Up-the-middle church can be amazingly bi-polar at times! I love it and hate it. I would do it for nothing, and wish I got paid more all at the same time. Being in the "people-building" business wears me out and pumps me up all in the same half-hour period of time. But there's nothing else in the world I would rather be spending my life doing. It's truly love/hate, in the purest sense of the phrase.

For example, today I wrote a kickin' message, and by the time I got to the office, was so discouraged by a few bad phone calls that I wanted to quit... *again.* We're in a business where we work our tails off for six straights days only to show up on the 7th day and find people who chose to prioritize other things like sleep, TV, football, or just forgot to come. What a crazy, bi-polar world church can be!

But still we do it. We wake up Monday morning, shred the latest copy of the resignation letter, go on a prayer walk, and face another week: A week where we get to invest in the lives of people. A week of ups and downs. Good phone calls and bad ones. A lot of days and weeks—its hard. But it's ministry and there's nothing else we'd rather do. It's hard, but it's the people business, and Jesus said it's the best thing going on the planet. To be a leader in a revolution that single-handedly has the ability to change the eternity of the entire planet. That's something I'm glad I get to give my life to.

The Challenge

The challenge for us, as pastors then, is not becoming jaded by the whole process. To maintain our emotions and spiritual centeredness to such a degree that we can actually lead this church into a greater reality. To not allow the programming to overwhelm us and push out the presence of God. To not allow the voices of people drown out the voice of God. To not allow the grueling pace of having to create an entirely new production every seven days drive us insane. To not allow the up-the-middle process to take the life from us.

I am confident that what you will find in the pages of this book will inspire you, encourage you, make you laugh, and challenge you to do this thing called church more effectively. What you hold in your hands is a collection of principles, stories, and ideas from a church that went up-the-middle and came out on the other side victorious!

I hope this book helps you enjoy the journey and recognize you're not alone. Up-the-middle churches are the new normal in the church world today.

Welcome to the up-the-middle reality of ministry,

Matt Keller

Section 1

The Practical Side of the Up-the-Middle Church

"...virtually all of the world's great companies were slow-brewed..."
- Your Marketing Sucks - Mark Stevens

Like great coffee, great churches are slow-brewed. There aren't too many churches today that get to launch with Pro Bowl quality players and state-of-the-art facilities in place from day one. That means the vast majority of us are going to have to figure out how to go Up the Middle in the practical aspects of our church. That's what Section 1 is all about.

Chapter 1

Building the Franchise

Up-the-middle churches leverage their brand to impact their community.

As a sports fan, I love flying into a pro sports city. The sport doesn't really matter to me. I just love knowing that a pro sport is happening there. From the moment I leave the plane, I can feel the excitement of the teams in town. T-Shirts, hats and, jerseys are available in the stores. Memorabilia hangs in restaurants and bars. Every city is crazy about their team! And the closer you get to the season, the more excitement you feel.

Great sports franchises don't just build great teams. They also build great brands in the community as well. A brand is the sum total of the reputation, thoughts and perceptions a sports team, business, or organization has among a group of people. The brand works in the community as a propeller of momentum for the team on the field. Great sports franchises and up-the-middle churches have this in common. Far beyond the weekly games or weekend services, a church's brand has the ability to generate momentum in the community.

How do we leverage that? How do up-the-middle churches make the most of their brand in the community? It starts by looking within to discover the defining characteristics of what you want your brand to be. It starts from the inside out.

14

The Purple Cow

I read a book called *The Purple Cow* by Seth Godin a few years ago. It's a simple 145 page read that will take you all of 90 minutes to get through. (It's worth it.) The big idea of the book is centered on an analogy of a "purple cow." Godin says if you and I drive through the countryside and see 2,000 black and white cows grazing on the hill side, we won't think a thing about it. But, if we see a purple cow standing in the field grazing next to the 2,000 black and white cows, we'll stop the car, jump out, grab a camera, take a bunch of pictures, and call all our friends to come and see it.

Godin contends that business (or in our case, church) is the same way. People will yawn and nod off at the same old, same old, but the minute we step out from the pack and give them something they have never seen before, that's the moment things begin to happen! He then challenges the reader to define their niche. (We'll talk about that later in the chapter.) The first step is to identify what sets you apart from every other entity like you.

Of course, in church work, we don't think in terms of competition with other churches. In fact, at Next Level Church, we have worked very hard to be *for* every church in our community. So rather than thinking in terms of *competition,* we must think *differentiation.* What are the things that make us different from every other experience in our attendee's week? What sets us apart? And ultimately, what will get people to pull the car over, grab a camera, and tell all their friends about what's happening in our church?

Finding NLC's Purple Cow

In the early days of Next Level Church, we knew a lot about what we *didn't* want to be, but very little about what we *did* want to be.

15

Therefore, defining our "purple cow" (or niche) was huge for us. After several hours of conversation, here's what we came up with: fun, casual, and passionate. Those are the three words we feel define us best. I'm sure there are others, but these are the three big ones. We want to aim with precision accuracy at these particular things. Let me unpack each one with a bit greater detail.

First, we want every environment we create to have an element of fun in it. We don't buy the idea that church has to be stuffy or boring in any way, shape, or form. I'm a pretty fun loving guy who suffers from ADD and hyperactivity, so things have got to move pretty quickly to keep my attention. I suppose we're creating a church that resembles that. Fun is a huge part of everything we do. From large group worship gatherings, to small group environments, we want there to be an element of fun involved. People can be serious anywhere. We try to push the envelope in the opposite direction. In short, I'd say we're serious about fun.

In 2008, we began using two of our pastors as the "Announcement Guys." It has brought freshness to an otherwise dull portion of our Sunday mornings. In fact, our people love the good cop, bad cop routine each week. Adding intentional fun to our announcements has made them a highlight rather than a drag to our Sunday morning experience.

In the summer of 2007, we had a tailgate party after church as a finale to our *Take Me Out to the Ballgame* series. It was a trip to see the parking lot full of people with swimming pools, smoker grills, and tents connecting in the parking lot of our high school after church! We even had one group bring a Winnebago. Infusing fun is huge for us!

Let me be clear, we're serious about what we do and in how we approach God. We're intense in encountering God but we also long to create a place that people enjoy coming to!

The second characteristic of our purple cow is "casual." In our minds, casual goes way beyond the clothes you wear. Casual for us is an attitude. We try and create a laid back, "come and see for yourself" experience at Next Level Church. From our coffee bar in the foyer to our approach to the challenge at the end of my messages, we work hard to let people know they can take this whole thing at their pace. The pressure is off. We're not rushing them, and neither is God. We're just really glad you're here.

Of course, we're casual in the way we dress too. At the end of the day, we're more concerned about hearts than clothes. We are trying to tear down barriers that keep people from experiencing God. The way you dress in a church can be one of those barriers. We believe God is more concerned with changing peoples' hearts, than He is with changing peoples' clothes. (After all, if He gets a hold of their heart, He could start working on their clothes after that, huh?)

Being in one of the hottest places on the planet (Southwest Florida) lends itself to people spending most of their waking hours in shorts and flip flops. We play to that. We know people will leave church and head to the beach or to their boat or to the park, afterward. We play to that reality. We could fight it, but why? I haven't found a scripture yet that says people can't come before God in their shorts and flip flops. We even had t-shirts printed up that read, "NLC, it's like Casual Friday, every Sunday!" just to let people know that we're cool with casual.

The third part of our purple cow is "passionate." This is the biggest one for us. People can go to a football game to have fun or go to a party to be casual, but a passion that changes their life can't be found at a football game or party. We're serious about encountering Jesus in a life-giving and life-changing way. We want passion to be infused into every environment of our church. From our corporate worship settings, to our kids' environments, to praying for one another in a small group setting, to conversations around bistro tables in our coffee bar area, we want people to sense and feel passion in everything we do and are! Passionate, fun and casual are three words that sum up the purple cow of our church.

So what's your purple cow? What are the characteristics that differentiate who you are from every other available option for your people in their lives? What will be those things that make people pull the car over, get out their cameras, and wait to see what happens next? Why should they come back to your church?

Identifying Your Audience (Making a "Most Likely to Attend" List)

Once you have established your purple cow, the next step becomes identifying your audience. By examining your purple cow, you can now begin to define characteristics of a group of people who are *most likely to attend* a church like yours.

Of course, at this point, someone will push back with the question of, "Doesn't Jesus say that we're not to exclude anyone?" Yes, and we shouldn't. By defining a *Most Likely to Attend* list, we simply attempt to be good stewards of what God has given to us. With limited resources, time, and manpower, it is necessary for every church to have a well-defined target to aim for. Otherwise, the church will spread itself too thin and end up doing nothing well. Too many churches struggle and flounder because they fail to find and define their audience.

When defining your audience, the goal is to know the characteristics of the people you are most likely to reach. Who are they? What do they identify with? What are they struggling with? What questions are they asking? What do they think of church in general? Identifying those characteristics will narrow your focus and increase your effectiveness in making an impact on your community.

I live in Southwest Florida. We are officially in the Tropics. In laymen's terms, that simply means it's hot most of the time. We have two seasons down here: Hot and Stinkin' Hot! Last week, while walking through Wal-Mart, I noticed an entire rack of wool scarves and winter gloves. I literally stopped in the aisle, looked down at the shorts I was wearing, and laughed out loud! Apparently, the executives at Wal-Mart don't understand this concept too well. (At least not the ones in the *winter apparel* department.)

In the same way it doesn't make sense for a store like Wal-Mart to designate large amounts of winter product to stores located in warm climates, it doesn't make sense for churches to designate large amounts of time, manpower, and money to areas outside of their niche. We've got to know our "most likely to attend" audience.

A great book that unpacks this concept is *Good to Great* by Jim Collins. In the book, Collins defines what he calls "The Hedgehog Concept." An organization that understands their hedgehog concept knows what they can be the best in the world at. I believe that chapter alone is worth the price of the book. It can help every church in defining its audience. (We actually studied this book chapter by chapter in the first year of our church. It was amazingly helpful.)

Searching for the Audience of Next Level Church

At Next Level Church, we understand our brand of Christianity isn't for everybody. We understand not everyone is going to prefer our style, but we are committed to helping people get plugged into a local church that's right for them. We are for every church in our community. We want to be the best in Southwest Florida at being fun, casual, and passionate. Then our goal is to find out what other churches in our area are *best in the world* at, so we can send people their direction. (We have helped many people get plugged into other churches across our community.)

Although we have a wide range of age groups represented in the family of NLC, we do have a specific target we aim at. What follows are a few statements that describe that target's worldview.

We think that those who are most likely to be looking for a church like ours:

- Are 18 - 45 year olds.
- Have young children.
- Don't think church is relevant to them in any way.
- Are familiar to the party scene.
- Are disillusioned with relationships and the dating scene.
- Care about spiritual things, but struggle with guilt.
- Are confused by a lot of the spiritual stuff that was pumped into them in parochial school.
- Are probably okay with the whole God concept, but have no clue that He isn't just "out to get them."
- Struggle with their self-image.
- Are caught up in quite a bit of materialism.
- Have very little clue of how to make wise financial decisions, but want everyone to think they have it all together.
- Are probably in debt and are contemplating leaving their job to find a better one.

When I read that list of characteristics, it makes my heart race! I desperately want to introduce those people to the love and grace of Jesus Christ! I want them to know they are not condemned or too far gone. I want them to know they are the ones Christ came to connect with most. I want desperately to create a place where they can come and feel accepted and connect with God in an authentic way! They are our target audience.

Designing Programming Around Your Target Audience

Once you've identified your target audience, designing programming begins to happen naturally. Up-the-middle churches design effective programs that serve their "most likely to attend" audience. Too many churches design programming based off past church experiences, not present day realities. *"We always had that..."* or, *"We did it that way in my last church,"* statements have no place in an up-the-middle reality. You don't have time to spend time, manpower, and money on programming for and from the past. Designing programming around the past will never create the optimal environment to reach people in the present or the future.

Knowing your purple cow and your audience, will affect everything you do—from how you structure your services (components and length), to how you design altar ministry opportunities. Achieving alignment in every area of your church will increase your effectiveness tremendously.

Let me challenge you to pull away with your key leaders for an extended period of time to consider how your programming ought to align with your purple cow and your audience. This was a huge lesson for us to understand. Once our programming came into alignment with our purple cow and our audience, interacting with the community took on a whole new meaning!

Moving from the Inside Out

Once a church defines its purple cow and audience and has a good handle on the alignment of the programming elements within church, the focus can begin to broaden to the community around it. This is where your brand come into play big time! Your brand can be defined as the summation of emotions connected to every interaction of your community with your church. (Wow, that was technical, sorry.) Let me explain…

We had only been in Southwest Florida for a couple of months when I remember telling our church planting team (all four of us) that *"Everything we do shapes the image of what Next Level Church will* *become in the future."* I wanted our team to know that from the first day we arrived in town, we began building our reputation, or the brand, of Next Level Church in the community.

This meant conversations, communication, and connection points with the community needed to be consistent. Consistency is huge when it comes to interacting with your community. The community is watching and testing everything they see and hear coming from the direction of your church. They want to know, *"Does this church come through and deliver on what they say they are going to do and be?"* Understanding the importance of consistency is key to creating movement with your church's brand in your community.

Understanding the Commitments of Our Brand

Since the beginning, we have been committed to a few "imperatives" in our interaction with the community. First, we are committed to being *for* every church in our city. We filter all of our communication with the community through the lens of one question: *"Could any of our language be construed **in any way** as competitive or negative toward another church?"* If our answer is yes *in anyway,* then we rework it completely. We never want to put down any other church.

It is our policy that we never tear down another church in our city. Do we see eye to eye on all the ways we do ministry? Of course not.

But whenever another pastor or church comes up in conversation, the first thing out of my mouth is something like, "That's a great church." Even if the person I'm with is dogging them. I will always come back with something positive that I've heard or seen from their church. (It's always a great plus to be able to tell people that I know the pastor or that he is a friend or acquaintance of mine.)

This is why we have never had any promotional material that drew attention to what we *weren't*. For example, "We don't spend money on big buildings," or "We're not stuffy and religious," or even "This ain't your momma's church." We never even want to have a hint of competition or condescension in our voice. We want to make sure the community knows we are for EVERY church! We continue to live by that today.

Second, we want our communication with the community to focus on the positive. We believe there is enough negativity in the marketplace. The last thing the world is looking for is condemnation of any kind. We want to be a church that accentuates the positive and focuses on the hope we have in Jesus Christ! We never want people to feel more acceptance at a bar than they do in our church. (After all, that's the real competition!)

A third thing we have been committed to is relevance. The danger of being in church work for a long period of time is the temptation to forget what it's like to be an un-churched person. What we *think* is important and appealing to an un-churched person, and what actually *is* important or appealing to an un-churched person are often two different things.

It is essential to attempt to climb inside the head of your niche. When it comes to promotional materials for our church, we try and aim at the un-churched person. So, if our aim is not church people, but un-churched people, then religious words just don't work too well.

A great filter we ask is *"What is this person facing?"* and *"What do they really want / need to know about our church?"* The average un-churched person reading our promotional materials probably cares less about our doctrinal statement and more about how to get to our meeting place. They're probably looking for answers to practical questions more than philosophical ones.

Being *for* every church, staying positive, and staying relevant are three keys to give your brand movement in interacting with your community. But building your brand goes deeper than just language and communication. The way you interact with other businesses and churches speaks volumes to your community as well.

Interacting Daily with the Community

Building your church's brand in the community has much to do with building a relationship with other businesses in your community. It entails day to day interaction with the businesses that make up your community. For example, when you get ready to purchase equipment for your church, why not buy it from a local retailer? Online purchasing is great, but no one from wherever.com will come to your church because you bought a projector from them.

Whenever possible, it's always a plus to purchase products and equipment from local retailers. (And most of the time, local retailers will match or get real close to any internet price you find anyway.) The on going relationship over time opens doors to show them an authentic side to our faith.

I recently ran into the owner of the largest guitar and music store in Southwest Florida. During our brief interaction, he went on and on about our programming director: what a great guy he was, and how easy he was to work with. That type of testimony is not only good for the brand of our church, but for the brand of Jesus Christ, as well.

Interacting with Other Pastors

In the region of the United States where I grew up, a lot of churches were extremely territorial. Pastors seldom ever met with one another, and when interaction did take place, it was guarded, shallow, and rather political. When we moved to Southwest Florida, we were committed to doing everything we could to meet and connect with as many pastors in the area as possible. I have a huge heart to see pastors working together to reach their community.

It's all about relationship. Since 2002, I have had the privilege of connecting with dozens of great pastors and leaders of other churches across our community. I have always tried to initiate those contacts whenever possible. This gives me the ability to affirm what they're doing and let them know right from the start that we are not here to compete with them in any way. I want the chance to communicate our heart to be on the same team, and we desire to send people their way whenever we can.

When it comes to connecting with other pastors, I want to be proactive rather than reactive. I always try and do as much homework as possible on the church before we meet. I try to have many positives to communicate about what they're doing. I certainly don't debate with a pastor in these meetings or question what they're doing.

I attempt to keep the focus on what we have in common. I share my heart and listen to theirs. I want the pastor to feel encouraged, like they have gained a friend, not a competitor by the end of the meeting. I am determined to listen more than I speak, and honor the pastors I meet and their commitment to the city. (Oh yeah, whenever possible, I try to pick up the check as well!)

I've never had one of these meetings turn out negatively. I've had a few lunches where we didn't really hit it off, and that was it. But by and large, it's always been a great experience to connect with as many pastors in my community as possible.

Referring People to Other Churches

The best benefit of being connected to other pastors in the community is that you can send people to them. At our Access NLC night, we tell people if after hearing our heart, they feel that Next Level Church is not the church for them, to not just leave. We invite them to come to us and let us help them find a church that might be a better fit for them.

We really believe our purpose isn't to build a great church, but to build people. If people feel they can be built up more effectively somewhere else, then we will **do** whatever we can to see that happen.

As an up-the-middle church, we can raise a new standard in our communities, regardless of what the church climate has been previously. With humility, we can bring the body of Christ together under the bigger picture of what God wants to do in an entire region of the country, not just in one church. (Somehow, I believe God is more glorified in that scenario, as well!)

We have had to live and die by this philosophy over the years. It hasn't always been easy to see families go somewhere else, but it's always been right and God has always honored us for our commitment to building His church in the city, not just our own.

Concluding Thoughts on Interacting with Our Community

Building the franchise of a church has everything to do with excellence and integrity. After all, we're not just building the brand of one local church but of the entire Body of Christ in our communities. Jesus said, *"If I be lifted up, I will draw all men unto me."* We want the community to know that when they interact with our church, they're connecting to a consistent, life-giving organization that values people and lifts up Jesus. That's a brand with attraction!

Chapter 1

Questions for the Huddle

Discussion Starters for Teams

1. What is the *Purple Cow* of your church? Spend time as a team defining exactly what it is that makes your church unique.

2. Who is the *Target Audience* of your church? Spend some time as a team making a "Most-likely-to-attend" list.

3. What are the tangible ways that your church is interacting with the community on a daily basis? Spend some time as a team talking about how you can be more strategic in building the brand of your church in the community.

Chapter 2

Life in the Locker Room

Up-the-middle churches create a culture for long-term success

Tony Dungy understands a little something about culture. Dungy has spent years shaping and molding the culture of the Indianapolis Colts organization from a mediocre football team, to Super Bowl champions. Dungy understands it is impossible to achieve success in the NFL, without first creating a culture of success around the organization.

Success doesn't just happen by accident. It comes by intentionally creating a culture of what will and will not be accepted practices in the locker room, on the practice field, and on game day. Creating a culture of faith and winning in the NFL doesn't happen by accident. It takes a distinct focus on the part of the leader. Tony Dungy embodies that type of focus.

Doing church up-the-middle is the same way. Church cultures don't just happen by accident. Every pastor must consciously engage the process of creating a culture that will bring long-term success in their church. Unfortunately, the talk about creating culture can get pretty philosophical if we're not careful. I've read several books on church culture and many struggle to pin the whole conversation to the ground. Let's talk culture in real terms… up-the-middle style.

Opening Up the Culture Conversation

When you talk about the *culture* of a business, restaurant, home, or church, you're talking about something that is more *felt* than *substantial* in most cases. Often the culture or feel of a church has more to do with the intangibles, than the tangibles. Why do we walk into some places of business and immediately feel dirty? Why do others draw us in and keep us there for hours? To answer that, you have to explore the concept of "felt sense."

Dr. Eugene Gendlin says in his book *Experiencing and the Creation of Meaning* that "A felt sense ultimately is the result of a myriad of tiny details that lurk somewhere below our conscious awareness. For example, without conjuring up specifics, the term *ice cream* is likely to bring about a very different felt sense from the word *vinegar.*" What's true of ice cream is definitely true of church. Since we began in 2002, we've learned a lot about the culture or *feel* that we want Next Level Church to have.

It takes time, energy, and intentionality over the long haul for a church to create the culture it desires: a culture that can produce a Super Bowl championship like the Indianapolis Colts have experienced, or one where people think *ice cream* more than *vinegar.* Here are some thoughts on how to do that.

Knowing That The Culture of Your Church Flows from Who You Are

In the fall of 2001, Sarah and I came to Florida to research Southwest Florida and connect with a few pastor friends of ours. One of those pastors we had lunch with was Bill Strayer, founding pastor of Calvary Chapel of New Port Richey, FL.

During our lunch together, we gleaned a number of principles from him—principles we continue to reference today. One of the most memorable things he said to us was this: "Within three years of your launch, your church will look just like you." I cannot tell you how true that is! It never ceases to amaze me to look across the church and see a reflection of us. I actually laugh at the fact that the median age of our church is exactly my age.

The principle is actually quite scary when spun in reverse. After the first few years, every pastor must face the reality that the quirks, flaws, or miscues in the culture of his church ultimately point back to him! (Ouch.) The single greatest influence on the culture of your church will be the senior leader! Of course, there are other influences that shape and mold the culture of your church, but by and large, the senior leader will be the driving force behind much of the culture that becomes your church in the future.

Understanding That People Take Their Cues from You

The first principle of creating culture is to understand the importance of your role as the senior leaders. People will watch you and create what they see you demonstrating, both consciously and subconsciously. In light of the three year mirror rule, my wife and I learned to let the environments of our church flow from who we were as leaders. We recognized that the people around us were taking their cues from us. Our launch team and others joining the church in the early days were taking their cues from us. They were attempting as best as they could to reflect the culture they saw us emphasizing and creating.

For the first couple of years of the church, we knew a lot about what we *didn't* want to be, but very little about what we *did* want to be. Unfortunately, this made it extremely difficult to articulate to the people around us the culture we did want to create.

31

In the early days, a lot of the cultural communication at Next Level Church happened through osmosis. We kept creating and casting vision for what we saw culturally, and then were very specific to veto and eliminate what didn't fit with the vision of the church. This wasn't always easy, but it was effective.

Since the church was just a few months old we have said we wanted to be the friendliest church in America. That has become a defining statement of the culture of our church. Our usher and greeter ministry now personally embodies the vision to make Next Level Church the friendliest church in America.

One of the most fulfilling experiences I have in my life is when I look around our church and see that it now looks the way we used to dream it could! Creating culture starts with the leader. Never underestimate your responsibility to model the kind of culture you want to have. People take their cues from you.

Seeing That Your Culture Is *As Much What You're NOT*, As It Is What You ARE

When I look back at our church in the early days, I still can't believe anyone actually came back. What we did then was so primitive compared to what we do today. When I talk to some of the people who are still with us from the early days, they always say the same thing: "*Back then, it was as much about what you* weren't *as it was about what you* were."

This is a valuable perspective for churches to grab a hold of. God has placed within us all a vision and dream of what our church will become in the future. All of those dreams are fantastic, and we must continue to pursue those with a vengeance. However, pastors and church planters, in particular, can buy themselves a few grace points simply by recognizing that what they *aren't* can be as appealing as what

32

This was my big Bol brov! 9/15

they *are*. This doesn't mean we don't strive for excellence in all that we do, and I'm certainly not advocating making excuses for a lack of attention to detail. What I am saying is when your church is small or young, it's just not possible to create everything you dream of in your heart.

Never underestimate the power of relationship, personality, and authenticity. Remember in a small context, or when your church is young that you are the chief representative of the culture. People will see and feel the culture by what they see and feel in you. When you are approachable, personable, and available, people will be drawn to that, even if all the bells and whistles aren't there yet. After all, it's not about the bells and whistles as much as it is being real.

I remember when our church was about two years old, one Sunday our drummer didn't show up, the movie theater made us move our coffee bar to one "shelf" and my message stunk bad. I turned to my wife as we were loading up and said, "I wouldn't come back to this church." To which she said, "Remember, people aren't coming because we're all of that. They're here because of what we are: real, honest and authentic." She was right. (She's always right!)

Cultural Pushback

Unfortunately, this type of thinking concerning the culture of your church in the early days can have backlash as the church grows. For example, a person who says they like your church because "it's not big" could conceivably begin to dislike it as it grows. (Trust me, you'll hear that.) They have mistaken size for culture. I always try to explain to people that the culture of our church will not change as we grow larger. I try to help them understand that the number of people any attendee can actually *know* is about twelve, no matter how big or small the church is. That is why we have small groups: so everyone has the ability to be known, no matter how big the church gets. (Sometimes they get it, sometimes they don't.)

Regardless of size or age, the culture of your church is built on what you're *not* as much as it is built on what you *are*.

Using Your Story to Communicate Culture

One of the best ways to shape the culture of your church is to use your story. Talking about what has shaped your view of Christianity and the church can bring amazing clarity for the culture of your church. Talking about the defining moments that have shaped who you are in your faith draws pictures of the type of culture you're trying to create in your church. Talking about the people who have influenced your spiritual journey allows people to construct mental images in their mind of the culture you're trying to create. I love to tell stories. They communicate heart in picture form. Stories can say what principles and vision statements never can. Use stories to communicate culture.

Jesus was a master story teller. He understood like no other leader ever has the power of a compelling story to shape the thinking of his followers. The disciples got used to hearing Jesus break into story at the most inopportune times. From the Good Samaritan to stories of farmers and prodigals, Jesus knew how to use stories to shape the culture and vision of those listening. And His stories continue to shape the vision of the movement of Christianity today.

Using Scripture to Communicate Culture

Another great way to shape culture in your church is through Scripture. I take every opportunity to shape the culture of our church during my weekly messages. I often use stories from Scripture to communicate the kind of church we want to be. I may slip it into a point by simply saying, "At Next Level Church we want to be the kind of church that…" Or we may do an entire series on our core values or one core value.

The Bible is filled with stories where a particular principle or cultural attribute was lived out and impacted on someone's life. Making the correlation between the Scripture and your church makes catching the culture simple for people. For example, if serving others unconditionally is a cultural piece of your church you want to emphasize, then preach on stories like the Good Samaritan. If you want your church to be known as a generous church, then teaching on passages such as the widow with two mites is a great way to communicate the culture you're attempting to create.

Developing a Language and Painting a Picture for People

As I've mentioned previously, in the early days, we knew a lot about what we didn't want to be, and very little about what we actually wanted to create concerning the culture of our church. In addition to modeling the culture we wanted, one of the best ways for us to communicate culture was to find places or examples of how we dreamed church could look, and then point our people to it.

For us, this happened with Northpoint Community Church in Alpharetta, GA. As you'll hear more in chapters four and five, when we locked on to what Andy Stanley and Northpoint were doing, we quickly had a model for how we dreamed church could look.

The key for many pastors is developing the skill of **translating down** what they see in the big guys. Unfortunately, many pastors of smaller churches find examples of what they dream of, but never translate the model or principles down to a smaller scale for their own reality. They immediately say, "*We could never do that*," or "*I wish we had a building*

/ budget / or staff to do that." Consequently, they remain paralyzed in their present state, unable to apply what they see for their people.

For example, when our church was just a couple of years old and still in the movie theater, we saw a long-bomb church with TV's in their foyer. We knew that as a smaller, mobile church, we would have trouble doing what they did, the way they did it. But that didn't stop our team. After a few weeks of dreaming, sketching and building, we were able to unveil three 19" flat screen TV's on bistro tables that provided a cool technological edge to our foyer environment. That is just one way we leveraged the art of translating down an idea from a "big guy."

I love that kind of thinking. At Next Level Church, we have a phrase we say often (I think I will put it on my tombstone someday). We say, "*We're church planters. We make it up. We figure it out. That's what we do. Don't tell me it can't be done.*" It's possible to glean principles and ideas from the big guys; it just requires the additional step of asking, "*What could that look like in our smaller context or mobile reality?*" Never let lack of money, resources, or options stop you from creating the culture you want to create.

Celebrating Positives When You See Them

Nothing reinforces culture like celebration. I have heard it said often that "*What gets rewarded, gets repeated.*" Take every opportunity you can to celebrate people living out the culture you desire to create in your church. Others will quickly notice and get on board as well. Finding people in your organization who are modeling the culture you desire to create is a great way to teach others what you're looking for. Seize that God-given opportunity.

9/07/15

Being Willing to Protect Your Culture

Protecting the culture of your church requires having some hard conversations. I remember in the early days of our church having to do this on several occasions. As a new or small church, you inevitably have some well-meaning Christians who begin attending but have a preconceived idea of what *they* think church should look like. When they see that your church doesn't look or feel like they think it ought to, at first they'll just chalk it up to a fluke or exception to the rule. But soon, they realize this is an intentional part of the culture you're attempting to create, and that's when the vocal fireworks begin to ignite.

In those moments, you'll feel the temptation to bend or compromise your culture in order to appease or keep those people. After all, if they've been around church for a while, they are probably those who give or those who tithe. That will make the temptation even greater. However, protecting the culture you feel led by God to create is your responsibility.

I remember so many e-mails and phone calls all beginning with the statement, "At my old church..." It was in those moments that the true culture of Next Level Church emerged. It's not really a core belief until you're willing to die for it. I have had to "die" on several hills in order to protect the culture of Next Level Church over the years.

For example, we have never had it in our heart to be a flag-waving church. I'm not personally opposed to flags in church. In fact, I have attended some great churches who have flags on their walls or use flags during worship. But for the culture we're attempting to create at NLC, we knew from the beginning that flags wouldn't work.

In the early days of our church, we had a couple of people ask about flags and we had to take a stand on the issue right away. They left and that was okay. In an up-the-middle reality, decisions like these are foundational in shaping the culture of your church. They will not be easy, but they will be the defining moments you look back on either with regret or gratitude. Moments I'm glad I didn't back away from now.

Avoiding Sacrificing the Masses for the Sake of the One

When it comes to protecting the culture of your church, it's vital not to sacrifice the masses for the one. This could prove to be one of the most difficult decisions you'll ever have to make in leading your church. However, failing to do this could end up causing you to lose the masses and keep the one. I know this may run cross-grained to conventional thinking, but when it comes to protecting the culture of your church, many pastors miss it. Because of pressure or desperation, too many pastors compromise the culture of their church in order to accommodate an individual or small group of people. Consequently, they end up losing the masses and keeping the small group.

For example, when our church was about three years old we had a woman who came in with a tambourine. She was a rather boisterous and outgoing worshipper, and her tambourine made her stick out even more. Put her in a room with stadium seating, and suddenly this woman had a crowd. I noticed that no one else was able to worship when this woman was worshipping. By the third week, I had several people writing me e-mails and calling me asking what we were going to do about this woman. They knew it wasn't the culture they had bought into.

Ultimately, I had a choice to make. My associate, Mike, ended up having the tough conversation with her. That was the last time we saw her. However, countless NLC attendees thanked us for protecting the culture we were trying so hard to create.

Sometimes decisions like this one can be difficult to make, but we can learn a lesson from Baskin Robbins. Baskin Robbins has thirty-one flavors for a reason. We understand not everyone enjoys the same flavor. We feel led to create a Chocolate Chip Cookie Dough culture. We understand not everyone wants that flavor, but that's who we are, and we have to fight for the integrity of our flavor of ice cream. Our culture won't be for everyone, but we are committed to Chocolate Chip Cookie Dough. So we feel confident to say, "Our flavor might not be for you, but there are other churches with that flavor..."

I realize this is easier said than done, especially when the people who challenge your culture are key leaders. The best I can say is have courage and protect your culture for the sake of the masses. It will be worth it in the end, and it will establish your leadership in the minds of the people who do get your culture.

Realizing That Your Culture Will Become an Automatic Filter

The greatest benefit of all that emerges from fighting for the culture of your church is the automatic filter it creates. When the culture of your church begins to permeate everything you do and are, people will automatically be drawn to it or resist it. Your culture will become a filter for your church.

For example, if the culture of your church is successfully communicated in your website, people will get a feel for your church long before they ever step foot into a weekend environment. The culture you communicate on your website will shape their expectations before they ever arrive to check you out. We have found that when people's expectations are met, they are more likely to return, even if they didn't *like* everything that happened. They'll come back just because their expectations were met. That's the power of culture.

Remaining Culturally Secure

Though the culture of your church shouldn't change drastically as you grow, the truth is, the dynamics of your church inevitably will. My friend Jack Wolfe, who pastors a church in northeast Atlanta, made this statement to my wife and I just before we moved to Florida: *"The level in which a person begins attending your church, will always be how they see it."* We have seen this come true over and over again. Here's an example.

If a person began attending your church when it was fifty people, in their minds, they're likely to always view it as fifty people. Consequently, when it grows to 100 or 150, they may begin to think or say, *"It's just not the same anymore,"* which, in their minds, is true. They may feel that your accessibility to them is diminished. Or that more people are requiring more of your time.

In year five, there was a woman who had been attending since the beginning. She was in for surgery and when my associate, Mike, went up to visit her, she communicated that she was highly offended that I (the senior pastor) had not come up to see her. Unfortunately, even after Mike attempted to communicate to her our logic and heart behind the decision, she still left the church. In debriefing on the incident, we were reminded that she had come into our church when it was about fifty people. Consequently, she had been unable to transition her mindset effectively with the growth of the church.

The goal for us as leaders is to help these people transition in their minds. Try to explain that the culture of the church isn't changing, just the dynamics of the church. However, the truth is, as John Maxwell says, "Not everyone is intended to take the whole journey with you." Love them graciously. But allow them the freedom to find another church. We have assisted people several times since we began in 2002 in finding another church. It will be difficult, but try not to take it personally. That's not always easy, but keeping your heart right is always the best road.

There have also been many who have made the transitions with us. This is why being intentional about creating an accurate culture in your church is so important. With the right culture in place, people will become attached to that, as much as they are to anything or anyone else in your church.

Concluding Thoughts on Creating Your Church's Culture

The conversation of culture is an abstract one. And yet, the culture you create in your church will be one of the most powerful tools you have to attract and keep people in your church. Let me close with a quote from Joseph A. Michelli, author of the book *"The Starbucks Experience"* concerning the unique culture that Starbucks has created in their stores around the world. He writes, "A competitive advantage occurs when everyone in a company appreciates that nothing is trivial and that customers notice everything."

Attendees notice everything. People will size up your church based as much on how they *feel* when they walk in, as they will on anything else you do. Winning games on the field begins with a culture of excellence in the locker room. When people think of your church, let's work hard to make sure they think of your flavor. That's the power of culture.

EVEN WHEN WE Are small talk ABOUT where you Are going

Mission Vision Statement

Chapter 2

Questions for the Huddle

Discussion Starters for Teams

1. Can you clearly define the culture of your church? Spend some time as a team discussing the cultural non-negotiables of your church.

2. What tough conversations are you going to need to have as a team in order to protect the culture of your church?

3. How can you celebrate examples of where people are living out the culture of your church?

Chapter 3

09-07-15 *Hyping the Big Game*

Up-the-middle churches use marketing and buzz for strategic advancement

Anyone who has ever played organized sports knows the hype that comes with the build up to a big game! In some cases it begins weeks before the actual event happens. Every great coach knows how to build the buzz! The greatest of coaches knows how to leverage tremendous amounts of creativity so his team is ready to play on game day.

The same can be said of church. Learning to market and create buzz around what God is doing in your church takes creativity and strategy. But how does that look in a new or smaller church context? What about budget and dollars? How can you get the most bang for your "buzzing buck?" With so much to lose as a new or smaller church, can we really afford to risk it with *buzz?* Mark Hughes said in his book *Buzzmarketing*, "Only when you've got everything to lose do you really understand the need to think differently. Without the fear of God, you tend to tread the familiar paths." Doing church up-the-middle requires leaders to think differently about how they create buzz and start conversations in their church and community. After all, there is never a week that goes by that we don't remind ourselves that today will be the day when someone will walk in the doors of our church and give God one more chance. We truly do have everything to lose, and that everything is souls.

Thinking Differently

That's really what the up-the-middle church is all about. For every church leader, it involves leaving security, comfort, and familiarity. Letting go of what has been to embrace what could be! We think that church can and should be different, right? We long for a church that doesn't resemble anything else we've seen before. We long for a clean slate: a clear canvas where God can show up and write on the hearts of people in a new way. Thinking differently requires harnessing the power of marketing and buzz.

Seeing a Growth Curve in the Arena of Marketing

In the first year of our church, I began to realize there was an untapped well in the realm of marketing we weren't taking full advantage of. Because we were meeting in the movie theater, we had unassumingly taken on the identity of *The Church in the Movie Theater*. That brand image had helped position us uniquely in the community, and good things were happening. The testimony of our church in the community was very positive. But I felt like something was missing. I knew we weren't optimizing the opportunity God had given us to truly establish the brand of Next Level Church in the community.

For the next year, I read everything I could get my hands on in the arena of marketing. I knew there was a great big marketing world out there I knew nothing about. What I began to learn fascinated me and I found that much of the information was immediately transferable into our church context. The concepts below changed how we approach buzz in our church and can change your church as well.

Creating Buzz

Mark Hughes defines Buzz as, *"capturing the attention of consum* *and the media to the point where talking about your brand or company becomes entertaining, fascinating, and newsworthy."* We realized at a year in, that is exactly what we needed to do. We needed to create a momentum that could entertain, fascinate, and get people talking. We wanted to put this car in motion so we could steer it in the direction God was calling us to go. I knew if we wanted to impact the community, we had to start with the inside first.

Creating Something from Nothing

Being a church plant forced us to realize we were creating something from nothing. Moving to an area with few resources, starting from the ground up, and making things up as we went helped us to realize the enormity of this principle. The greatness of a church plant is found in the **lack of pre-conceived ways of doing things.** There are no rules or stipulations that contain you. The downside is it means you really do have to make everything up as you go.

At every turn we had to create momentum. In an existing church setting, momentum already exists. It might not be as strong as one would like, or might not be pushing people in the right direction, but it does exist. The car *is* moving. It might not be moving in the right direction, but there is movement. There is a tremendous difference between the energy involved in turning a car that is stopped and turning a car already in motion.

As church planters we didn't have the luxury of the car being in motion. It felt like we were trying to turn a car that was sitting still. In those moments, we had to figure out how to get the car rolling, and le right direction. That's how we learned about

[handwritten: Weekend service must Be Awesome! (God is on display)]

[handwritten margin notes: Promote new series Two weeks out]

[handwritten margin notes: 09% we have Promotionally changed this the last 3 weeks]

...ed studying marketing and buzz, we began to realize that our Su.. / morning product had to improve. This is a constant battle for church leaders. What happened on Sunday mornings had to become predictable, excellent, and buzz worthy, or people would never feel comfortable inviting their friends. We had to get to a place where we could be trusted by the people of our church. I believe the speed at which a church can create a consistent, life-giving, and predictable environment in their Sunday morning product is directly proportional to the speed at which they're capable of numerical growth.

There were many elements that led to our creating a predictable environment in our Sunday morning product, from worship style, sound and lighting, start and end times, to things like the foyer and kids' environments. (We'll talk more about that in the *Creating the Game Day Experience* Chapter.) We learned everything mattered, and on an internal buzz level, we knew we had to give more attention to the creative elements of our services. The goal of buzz is conversation. If you can get your people having conversations about your church, buzz is happening.

Promoting Every New Series

The central creative element every church has is the message series. We create buzz around every new series we do. Some more than others, but every series is promoted in advance. Ideally, two weeks before we begin every series, we'll start building buzz about it. Our series usually last between three and six weeks. We refer to this as the *GAP* principle.

The clothing store *GAP* changes its look every six weeks. (And they've been pretty successful, right?)

There are all kinds of ways to do this, from simple bulletin or stage announcements to handing out a creative element or sending out a promotional e-mail. They can be simple or complex and as inexpensive or costly as you want. The hope is, by the time we get to the series, we have people saying, "I can't wait to hear what we're talking about!"

Three times a year we do a huge "pull-out-all-the-stops" series. Every NLC attendee knows these are the best times to invite their unchurched friends and co-workers. Our *big series* are starting to take on a whole reputation of their own. Our people know when we start promoting them that it's going to be crazy!

Getting and Staying Ahead in Message Prep

In order to buzz a series effectively, it takes planning and foresight—getting ahead in your message preparation. Saying it and actually doing it are two different stories, though. Let's face it—life happens, and in the ministry, life happens unpredictably fast. You have to be able to rise above the weekly grind and think about what's going to be happening in six or eight weeks. It also means that, as the lead communicator in your church, you have to have a general handle on where you want the church to go long before you get there. I often hear pastors talk about how difficult it is to *get ahead* in their message preparation. Personally, I believe it all comes down to how we think about it.

Most of us come by a mindset honestly from our old-school experience and Bible college professors. This mindset says, "If it's going to be fresh and anointed, it's got to be last minute." Again, quite honestly, for many of us (myself included), we love the rush of adrenaline and anointing that comes from God showing up in the eleventh hour on Saturday night and giving us a word, don't we? If we'll admit it, some of us believe our best messages ever have been produced like that, haven't they? So then why is it such a bad strategy for our churches?

The answer lies in the difference between two Thanksgiving turkeys. Your mother could warm up a turkey dinner in the microwave. It would be edible, but we all know it would taste better if she let it cook in the oven for about four hours. The same is true with message preparation. In order to deliver nutrition and health over the long-term, it's necessary to learn to cook our messages, not just microwave them. People in our culture today have come to know the difference.

One of the benefits of the slow-roasted message is generating time for creativity. Before I was able to get ahead in my message preparation, a great creative idea would emerge, but we wouldn't have the time to execute it. Consequently, many great ideas died on the table for no other reason than the failure to plan. Now that I stay ahead of message preparation, we have ample time to dream up, think about, and execute creative, memorable, and buzz-worthy concepts.

If we never get past life in the moment, we'll simply rush from week to week in preparation and short sell our people. They end up with microwave dinners that could have been Thanksgiving feasts. However, if we'll take the time to begin planning out general message series and concepts for messages weeks and months in advance, we'll end up serving more nutritional meals that are better tasting, better for them, and are worth buzzing about to others!

In order to improve the buzz factor in your church, here are some simple recommendations for getting and staying ahead. First, determine that it's *that* important. Unfortunately, creativity for many of us ends up being optional. We think, *"If I have time, I'll try and think up something creative to do."* So the first step is to change our perspective about it. If it truly is the creative elements that get people talking and generate buzz, then it's vitally important to prioritize those into our weekly agenda.

A couple of years back, I became addicted to the giant Post-It notes you can buy at office supply stores. My life has been forever different because of them. Today, if you come into my office, you will find these great white, "post-it's of love," pasted all over the walls and windows! They give me the ability to see things in larger-than-life view. (I can't do small paper anymore, I have to see it big!)

We have a *White Board Year of Sundays* that hangs my outer office. I'll block in important dates and events that are coming up, such as Easter, Christmas, or Spring Break. We also fill in what other things are happening such as our newcomer's receptions, water baptisms, or Access NLC type classes.

By looking at the Sundays in long view, I'm able to begin to see the rhythm of the calendar emerge. This clues me into how the weeks of a series might begin to look, or when the best time for my vacation might be. It gives me the ability to adjust things in real time, long before we ever get to the individual Sunday. This white board of Sundays and the Post-it notes have been the single greatest factor in helping me get ahead in my message preparation.

Second, you've got to schedule some "Flat Tire Time." Allow me to explain. Our associate pastor, Mike Ash, actually made up the term "Flat Tire Time." A few years back, Mike was getting frustrated with the busyness of his weekly schedule. Essential things in his week were being pushed out by urgent and unimportant things. Then he had a tire blow on his car.

For the next two hours, whether he wanted to or not, he had to deal with fixing that tire. He cancelled appointments, neglected phone calls and e-mails, and stopped everything. Why? Because if he didn't fix the tire, he wasn't going to be able to go anywhere. The flat tire immediately took first place in his life.

In that moment, Mike discovered that making time *was* possible; he just needed to change his perspective. So now, he schedules "Flat Tire Time" for the things that are most important. So , we've adopted his language and it has worked beautifully. (By the way, I'm always amazed at how many of the other urgent things seem to miraculously get done anyway. It's incredible how non-essential things become when we begin prioritizing the truly essential.)

A third recommendation for upping the creative buzz factor in your Sunday mornings is to get others involved in the process. I learned early on in doing church up-the-middle that I was going to need help in coming up with "Buzzable" ideas. I'm blown away by the insights and ideas that come from the most unique people in our church when I simply invite them in to the process. Simply shooting out an e-mail to different types of people in different age groups can generate amazing results! People come up with movie clips, visual aids, real life stories, etc. Inviting others into the process gives them ownership as well. (Another factor that gets people talking.)

A final thought comes from Andy Stanley's book, *Communicating for a Change.* He says the easiest way to get ahead in message prep is to schedule a guest speaker for two weeks in a row. Then prepare during your week as normal. By the end of the two weeks, you'll be three weeks ahead in your message preparation. Brilliant! If you can't afford to bring in someone from the outside just use one of your associates or key leaders.

I can't tell you the freedom and fun that begins to come when the, "Monster of Sunday" isn't nipping at your heals all week long. I find that I'm in a better mood during my day because I'm not worrying about what I'm talking about. Then, my weekly study time becomes about writing a message for the future and reviewing and finalizing the message for this weekend.

Generating Buzz by Giving

We love giving stuff away. We are so appreciative and thankful for the people of our church, and we are constantly looking for every opportunity we can find to bless them. Tying it into a series gives it an even greater punch! In the fall of 2006, we did a series called *"The Big Gulp...Increasing Our Spiritual Capacity."* On the first weekend, we gave away 44 oz. souvenir Big Gulp cups to everyone as they walked in. We stuffed our bulletins and offering envelopes inside, and our people loved it! We also gave all of our ushers, greeters, and worship team free *Big Gulp* t-shirts to wear throughout the entire five weeks of the series. Again, our people loved it.

When our church was just nine months old, we were introduced to a church planting organization that has truly changed our philosophy of ministry. The organization is the Association of Related Churches or ARC. The ARC is a champion of the "free stuff" philosophy. They truly embody a spirit of generosity. The annual conference they hold each year for all of their pastors and church planters is absolutely free! It's not just for lead pastors either. Churches are encouraged to bring as many people as they want. The heart behind the organization is to create a culture of generosity that becomes contagious. That filters down into the churches of the ARC, as well. It is a privilege to pass down that heart into the people of Next Level Church! (For more information about the ARC check out www.ARCChurches.com.)

Giving People a Reason to Come Back...and Bring Someone with Them!

At the end of the day, "buzz" is about giving people a reason to come back next Sunday! If you can get your people saying, *"I can't wait to see what will happen next!"* then you're creating buzz effectively. When you start creating buzz around your weekend services, you will begin to feel momentum starting to build. When that happens, your church will begin to grow!

External Buzz

Once your Sunday morning product begins moving toward consistency, the next step is to turn your sights outward to an external level. Here are a few thoughts on creating buzz in the community.

Learning the Need to Create a New Category

In a book called *The Fall of Marketing and the Rise of PR,* by Al Ries, buried deep in the pages of an otherwise rather ordinary book, is one of the coolest little concepts we found pertaining to buzz. Ries contends that the best way to generate buzz in a community or organization is not by simply doing something everyone else is already doing, or just doing it a little better or different. Buzz is actually generated by *creating an entirely new category!* The first time I read that, it nearly jumped off the page at me. Let me explain.

A pastor friend of mine was in the throws of opening a child care facility in his church. He came down to visit for a few days, and we were reading the book together. One of the main objectives of his trip was to brainstorm about possible names for his child care facility. So the minute I read that, I asked him the question, "What is it that your child care facility will actually do? If it's not in the day care category, then what is it?"

9/15

we want to help people live their lives w/ Jesus @ the center!

The Up the Middle Church

After about fifteen minutes of prodding, he finally articulated it. He said, "Well, we're in the business of partnering with parents!" And suddenly a new category was born, just as Al Ries had written! They weren't opening a day care; they were partnering with parents in developing young lives. What a brilliant and valuable distinction.

Now what does this "creating a new category" idea necessarily have to do with church? I think far too many pastors see themselves in the wrong business. They think they're out to build a church. If we take this concept to heart, what we learn is that we're not in the church building business; we're in the people-building business. The minute we were able to articulate that small, but powerful distinction, it changed how we approached everything we did in our church!

Suddenly, we weren't just using people to build church programs. We were using church programs to build people. Instead of seeing people as a means to an end, we now saw people as the end in and of themselves! Our highest priority was on the individual, not just the process or program. It was a huge insight for us.

we make programs for people, not people for programs

The man of God destroys symbols

Finding Your Key Times and Exploiting Them

About three times a year, we try and prioritize growth and outreach into the community. In every calendar year, in every community, there are key times to invite the community into what is happening in your church. Take advantage of those. The times may vary depending on the region of the country you're in, but they do exist in your community's yearly rhythm and calendar. Pastors who understand the power of buzz don't miss them.

This is something we learned early on, but didn't always do a great job of executing. In the early days, we missed some amazing opportunities to get the word out about Next Level Church simply because we weren't prepared for these key times.

Back to school is a big time for families in setting their priorities for the year. Take advantage of letting parents know that a renewed commitment to regular church attendance can be one of those big rocks they put into their family schedule. We usually prepare for a big fall push around back-to-school time.

Easter is another obvious one. However, our experience with Easter has been that there is a steady decline from Easter to Memorial Day and the end of the school year. We will usually launch a new series on Easter that ends somewhere near the third week of May for that reason. By Memorial Day, people are checking out and heading for Disney World or up north.

In most places, Christmas is big. However, our experience has been a bit atypical. Most of the Christmas promotion we've done in the past ends up getting swallowed up in the other festivities of the holidays. Southwest Florida is quite transient, as well, so many of our attendees are away around the holidays. On the other hand, Ed Young Jr., pastor of Fellowship Church in Dallas, TX, says that the biggest outreach of the year for their church is Christmas Eve.

Every region of the country will be different. You'll have to discover the rhythm to your calendar as you go. The key is getting and staying ahead so you can make the most of the opportunities you have!

Designating Money to Marketing

One draw back to church planting similar to our experience is that, as the new church in your community, no one knows you're there. Compound lack of awareness with a new church's mobile reality and, the young church has two strikes against it right away. Getting people buzzing about your church becomes more important than ever. Ultimately, that will require money.

One of the great things we learned from the ARC was to set the precedent of designating percentage points of our budget for marketing and outreach from the beginning. If you build it in when you are small, it will be a huge plus as your budget grows! The ideal is 10%. Think of the creative elements you could employ to create buzz in your church and community if you had 10% of your budget designated to do it? I would highly recommend to any church going up-the-middle to begin building that priority in now. Even if you can't do 10%, start somewhere.

A major benefit to setting budgetary percentage points aside each year is that it takes the emotion of the moment out of it. Instead of getting to a key time and thinking, "*Oh no, where are we going to find that much money to give to this mailer, campaign, or giveaway?*" the money will already be there. No need to freak out. Just spend what you already have budgeted.

Another benefit is the ability to dream big. When you know you have several thousand dollars this year to spend on marketing and buzz, you'll naturally think bigger. I always tell our team to dream as if money is no obstacle. Then, we simply have to find a cheaper way to create the same result! (Which is almost *always* possible!) The tendency of marketing is to get locked into the here and now, simply because of the "Monster of Sunday." Setting aside money in advance gives your mind permission to think ahead. Take advantage of that.

Differentiating the Two Types of External Marketing

When it comes to marketing and creating buzz in your community, there are really only two basic types. The first type is *Brand Awareness* marketing. Brand Awareness has to do with letting the community know you exist. "*Hey, we're a church, we're pretty cool, and we're here if you're looking for one...*" type of stuff. Banners on Little League signs, general newspaper ads, etc. are great for this type of thing. Advertisers refer to having a *Top of Mind* Awareness in your community. When they think about church, who do they think about? Brand Awareness marketing does that for you.

The other type of marketing is *Call to Action* marketing. Call to Action Marketing has a desired action step built in. It goes beyond Brand Awareness and actually invites people to do something about it. For example, "*Come to church on Easter Sunday!*" or "*Come to the Fall Kickoff of blah blah blah...*" You're actually asking people to take a step.

This type of marketing is effective because it gives people something to be apart of. The downside to this type of marketing is that once the event or date is passed, they may not think about it again. For example, the Christian school my kids attend hosted a Fall Fun Festival on a Saturday. When I received the flyer, I thought it might be something fun to attend. What I didn't think was, "Maybe we should go to their church on a Sunday."

Jesus would have called *Brand Awareness* marketing, "seed sowing" opportunities, and *Call to Action* marketing, "reaping opportunities." He understood this concept completely. So must we. The most important thing about your marketing will be to know and remember your purpose.

National companies have the capital to do a lot of Brand Awareness marketing. They can afford to just *be* places like outfield fences that don't necessarily call people to action. However, in a local church setting, we have far less dollars to get the word out. Make them count. Always ask yourself, "What are we hoping people will do with this information?" That will bring focus and clarity to your marketing campaigns.

Concluding Thoughts on Marketing and Buzz

When it comes to marketing and buzz, never forget that Sunday is what you're doing. It's where the vast majority of your resources and time and energy are being spent. The most important thing you can spend your time buzzing is your Sunday mornings. Marketing around your Sunday morning will position your church for the greatest amount of return.

When you begin by thinking differently about what business you're in, and begin harnessing the power of buzz both internally and externally, the results will be staggering. The key will be prioritizing the time and energy to make your Sunday morning product soar with consistency and give people a reason to come back. When people get excited to see what will happen next, they begin to bring others along with them. In that moment, eternity begins to change, one soul at a time—one Sunday at a time! Now that's something to buzz about!

Chapter 3

Questions for the Huddle

Discussion Starters for Teams

1. How effective are you being at creating buzz internally? Spend some time as a team discussing how you can give people a reason to come back and bring someone with them.

2. How effective are you being at creating buzz externally in the community? Spend some time as a team determining how you make the most of every opportunity to get the community talking about your church.

3. How strategic is your church's yearly calendar? Spend some time as a team talking about the three major growth seasons of your church.

Section 2

The Process Side of the Up-the-Middle Church

"A system is simply a strategic process that saves you stress, time, energy and money."

- Launch - Nelson Searcy and Kerrick Thomas

In an up-the-middle reality, process is everything.

Churches who can master their processes are well on their way to success!

That's what Section 2 is all about.

Chapter 4

Creating the Game Day Experience

Up-the-middle churches embrace an everything matters mindset

for game day.

The experience of a football game begins long before the fan arrives at his seat. Parking, signs, ticket booths, turnstiles, concession stands, souvenir shops, loud speakers, pre-game introductions, large projection screens, and friendly ushers. Every football franchise understands the hundreds of micro-components that go into creating a great fan experience at a football game. And then there's what happens on the field prior to game time...

There's nothing more fascinating to me than watching the warm up routine of a professional football team on any given Sunday. The kicker is practicing from both hash-marks at varying distances while the punter is kicking into the air, quarterbacks are practicing timing patterns with wide receivers, running-backs are rehearsing handoffs, linemen are running through blocking patterns. Even backup players are engaged in rehearsing plays on the off chance their number will be called upon later in the day.

Great football franchises know there are no unimportant elements when it comes to game day. Everything matters in football. Up-the-middle churches also have an *everything matters* mentality!

Everything Matters

I first came across the *Everything Matters* principle in the book *A New Brand World* written by Scott Bedbury, chief marketing executive for Nike and Starbucks. Bedbury tells the story of traveling through Africa with Starbucks CEO, Howard Shultz. The purpose of the trip was to examine the current practices their company was using in growing and harvesting the coffee beans used to produce their Starbucks coffee.

In the midst of one conversation Bedbury asked Shultz, "Of everything that goes into a cup of Starbucks coffee, what matters the most?" Bedbury records that Shultz paused for a moment, looked out the window at the African landscape and then replied, "Everything. Everything matters." He went on to say there isn't one piece of the process that *isn't* important in making a great coffee experience one cup at a time.

The same principle holds true in our churches — perhaps even more so. After all, we're not just creating environments where people can experience a great cup of coffee. We're creating life-giving environments where people can experience God first hand. An up-the-middle church makes it easy for the un-churched person to find their next step. We have come up with a "parking lot to parking lot" philosophy to encapsulate this value. The "parking lot to parking lot" philosophy centers around the idea that from the minute someone pulls into the parking lot to the time they drive off, they are under our influence. Everything matters.

Defining the Win

The "parking lot to parking lot" philosophy starts with defining the win. At NLC, we define a win as having the ability to influence people over an extended period of time. In short, our goal is to get people to come back. It's great to be able to speak into someone's life once, but we feel true life-change happens over time, not just with one shot. At NLC, we understand our Sunday mornings are the primary front door to our church. Over 90% of NLC attendees enter through our Sunday mornings. That means we've got to pay attention to every detail.

Minimizing Excuses

A second component of the "parking lot to parking lot" philosophy is minimizing the excuses. We understand there are a hundred excuses for a person not to come back to our church each week. Our goal, then, each week, is to eliminate as many of those excuses as we possibly can. There is no detail we don't try and have a handle on. We start in our parking lot, and move all the way through every environment of our Sunday mornings attempting to see it through the eyes of a new person. What do they see when they pull off the street? What do they need to know? How are they feeling at each moment? We try and put ourselves in their shoes at every moment of their time at NLC. We want to make it easy for new people to navigate through our foyer and coffee bar environments, our kid's environments, the restrooms, and the auditorium. If we can eliminate confusion for them by making things simple and easy, they're more likely to come back. And that's a huge win for us!

Experimenting in the "Parking Lot" Philosophy

I was talking to a pastor a few months back who was having trouble getting some of his key leadership to think about their church in terms of an un-churched or de-churched person. In the course of the conversation I said to him that I thought his leadership has forgotten what it's like to be a lost person. It has probably been too long since

each was a first-timer in a church. He agreed wholehearte
him the following recommendation...

Begin sending your leaders out, two couples each weel
churches in your community on a Sunday morning. Give them explicit
instructions to role play during the morning. In other words, they were
to visit the church with the mindset of young parents, a single person,
an older couple, or a single mom attending for the first time. Their
goal would be to force themselves to see the church through a new
person's eyes. Consider signage, distance to the front doors, locations
of the nurseries and restrooms, cleanliness of the facility, etc.

Then bring them back to your leadership meeting the following
week and talk about how they felt. Did they feel confused? Were
they nervous or intimidated? Did they feel out of place? Were things
difficult to find? What assumptions did the church make of their
newcomers? It was a phenomenal exercise in stretching his team.

Of course, the purpose of the exercise is not to critique a sister
church in the community in any way, but rather to give leaders a chance
to rethink the assumptions they're making about their own church.
Perhaps it's been too long since you or some of your key leaders have
been the new person. Using this strategy could cause you to see your
church through new eyes.

Getting out and Seeing the World

My recommendation for church planters in the pre-launch phase
is to keep your Sunday mornings available as long as you possibly can.
Once you start Sunday mornings, you can never stop them. In many
ways, it's like having a child. Once it's out of the womb, somebody has
to care for it for the rest of its life. If you're in that pre-launch phase,
hold your launch team meetings any other time than Sunday mornings.
Instead, spend your Sunday mornings traveling and seeing as many

other churches in action as you possibly can. Send out multiple groups to multiple churches in multiple cities every week if you can.

Have them take a video camera and digital camera with them to capture as many ideas as possible. Tell the church you're coming so they can give you complete access to the hows and why's of everything they do. (It will make most churches feel great that you've come to check out what they're doing and how they're doing it.) There are some amazing secrets hiding just beneath the surface of every church. Get in there and fish them out. It's worth it in the long run.

If you can have lunch with the pastor or another key leader on the team afterward, do it. Come prepared with all kinds of questions about *the why of the why*, behind everything they do. Do three times as much listening as talking in those meetings. (You're not there to tell them how great you're going to be; you're there to see where they are great and learn.)

Get back together with your team on Sunday night and talk through what you saw. Keep the ideas that fit your culture and throw out the ones that don't. The more exposure you can have to churches who are doing church the way you want to be doing it before you launch, the better position you'll be in for when you do launch.

If you're already doing Sunday morning church, getting out and seeing the world can prove to be a bit trickier. I personally think every pastor should be out of his or her own church at least four times a year. If you plan the morning right, you can see two or three different churches. Don't be afraid to take advantage of Saturday or Sunday night services as well. Seeing others keeps your mind fresh to what's happening in the church world around you.

It's worth mentioning that you can learn a lot about other churches through the internet, as well. Many churches have video feeds of their services. And most all websites have pictures of staging, classrooms, and coffee bar environments. A picture can speak a thousand words. Watching how others pay attention to everything can help you pay attention to everything, too.

Thinking About Several Key Areas in Your Church

Since beginning in 2002, we've learned a lot about the details and how everything matters. The following few pages are just a *short list* of some of the areas you'll want to make sure you don't overlook. The list is not exhaustive, but hopefully it will help you get the juices flowing as you think through your own church.

1. Restrooms

Just think about the last gas station restroom you were in. They matter, even if you're in rented space. Do whatever it takes to make them as appealing, clean, and professional as they need to be. A great target to aim for is to be on the equivalent of a Marriott or Hilton level hotel.

Shortly after we relocated to the high school, we discovered there weren't enough hand dryers in the restrooms. Rather than have people standing in line to dry their hands, we put paper towels in place for people to quickly wipe their hands and go. One church I know puts mints in their restrooms each Sunday just for a nice touch. Do whatever it takes to make sure your restrooms speak highly of your church.

2. Entry Points

Most churches have just one or two entry points in which every attendee passes through on a Sunday. Take advantage of these entry points. Staff them with lots of smiling greeters and guides to make people feel comfortable and welcomed. In the early days of our church,

Matt Keller

we used a nametag table as the initial touch point of our church. We had signs that said, "*Help us create a more relational environment by wearing a name tag. Thanks.*" It made it easy for anyone to talk to anyone and provided a safe place for our greeters to welcome new families.

After about five years, and right around the time we reached the 500 mark in weekly attendance, we discovered that the nametag table was more of a hindrance than a help. Today we have two *New Here?* Kiosks that serve as our first stop as new people enter the building. Each new person is greeted personally, given a map of the school, and escorted personally to the kids' zone if they have children. We want our new people to feel as special as they want to be. One advantage of giving new people maps is that anyone in leadership who sees someone walking through the foyer with a map immediately knows they're new and will move in their direction to greet them, assist them, and welcome them. Having a greeter team in the entry way that is adequately staffed is incredibly important.

A few weeks ago, before church began, one of our greeters introduced me to a lady who was visiting for the first time. As I introduced myself to her as the lead pastor, she responded that she already felt so welcomed. She said, "In the last five minutes, since I walked in, I've been greeted by five people, given a personal guide, who is now getting me a bottle of water, and introduced to the pastor. Wow. That's hospitality!" I simply responded to her, "That's what we're going for. We just want you to know that we're really glad you're here!" Take advantage of your entry points into your building and make it easy for people to find their way.

For the first couple of years our primary greeter system was Mike, our associate pastor, outside on the entry steps to the theater, my wife Sarah, on the inside, and then one greeter at the kids check-in. Today

66

we have over 60 greeters on our team. We have gone from three to sixty but the culture is same today as it was in the first few years.

3. *Coffee Bar*

[handwritten: FREE LATTES + WATER EVERY WEEK.]

Even though we're a mobile church, we have an entire team who sets up a coffee and donut bar each week. One of the core priorities for our church is relationship. We want to create a relational and laid back environment, and having free coffee and donuts each week does that for us.

Our coffee bar has morphed a lot since the early days of our church, but the one thing we've always strived for is that it be easy and free. The tables are laid out in such a way that lots of people can have access to what they need quickly and efficiently. We bring in kids' picnic tables complete with wet wipes on each table for easy clean up of both the tables and the kids. (We have found it's better for kids to sit and eat their donuts than run and eat their donuts!) Our parents love it!

Think through every detail. Think like the people you're trying to reach. Determine what environments you want to create, and then create them with excellence and ease.

4. *Signage*

One of the biggest things for a new person is simply knowing where they're going. Because we've been around our church for a while, it's easy to forget that new people don't know where they're going. We invest quite a bit of time, energy and money to create full-color, professional, and big signs that help people get where they need to go.

When we were doing church in the movie theater, we were competing with Hollywood caliber signs and posters all around us. Therefore, our signs had to be large and eye-catching, or else they would get lost in the sea of Harry Potter promotional items. We had no trouble spending $450 on a six-foot tall by three-foot wide full color sign that simply had our NLC logo on it and a big arrow pointing people where they needed to go. Now that we're doing church in a school, not only do we not have the competition for visual stimulation, but we've also got about eight times as much space to cover. I think we spent close to $5,000 on updating all of our signs from parking lot to parking lot when we made our move to the high school. Don't be afraid to invest in high quality, big signs that make it easy for people to navigate through your church location. People will never thank you for it, but it makes a world of difference.

5. Kids' Check-in

At the end of our coffee bar and foyer environment is our Kids Zone. Every child from infant through elementary has to check-in. This makes it easy for families with multiple kids. If a family is new, one of the kids' check-in greeters will escort them to each of the classes where their children will be that morning. They can introduce them to the teachers and workers and be sure the children *and* parents are comfortable. They then guide them to the auditorium and answer any other questions they may have about NLC or our kid's environments. Assume nothing.

6. Auditorium

Everything matters in the auditorium, as well. Twenty minutes before our Sunday morning service begins, we make sure the auditorium environment is set with hopeful music and inviting lighting. The stage is clear of musicians, etc. All microphone checks and other sound and lighting issues are dealt with before the doors are ever opened. Once people start coming into the auditorium, in their minds, the service has started. Anything unprofessional or incongruent is seen as a distraction to their overall church experience.

Being mobile doesn't mean you can get away with sloppy. Teach the excellence principle to everyone who is involved in making the Sunday morning environment happen. We have a mandatory production meeting thirty minutes before each service begins. It usually lasts about ten minutes. It simply gives everyone a chance to talk through what the big idea of the day is, and what we're hoping to accomplish in the hearts of the people in attendance. (Remember, there are 100 reasons for someone not to come back; we want to do everything we can to eliminate as many of those as possible.)

We also want everyone involved on a production level to have as much information as possible in their hands, to eliminate as many distractions as we possibly can. We never want to get in the way of God touching peoples' hearts. We know that if the air conditioner is too cold, or the lights are too bright at the wrong time, it can become a distraction for someone to encounter and hear from God like we are hoping them to do. Even when we had a hundred people in weekly attendance we had a production sheet. It just positions everyone involved for maximum success.

Let me play the other side of this for a minute. I heard Greg Surratt, the pastor of Seacoast Church in Charleston, SC (www.seacoast.org), say once that you have to adopt a good enough perspective. He went on to say that it's possible to get so obsessed with the details of a service, that you kill the spirit behind it. Do everything you can to make your services have fewer distractions. Communicate as much as you can with your team, but then put it in God's hands. If you don't, you end up making the desire to eliminate distractions a distraction itself.

EXcellent NOT PERFECTion

We tell our production team that service starts twenty minutes before we sing the first song, and it ends twenty minutes after we dismiss. We don't want to disrupt our auditorium environment during that entire time.

7. Kid's Environments

Obviously, if you intend to reach and keep young families, you have to have a strategy for ministry to the children. Having a conversation about your desired goals for building children, or *future adults* will position your church to not just baby-sit children, but grow them intentionally. In a resource-scarce environment like many churches find themselves in, too many times ministry to children is reduced to babysitting, or, at best, entertaining while the adults have real church.

It doesn't have to be this way. It's quite possible, even as a new or young church, to have a strategy in place to actually begin developing the spiritual lives of children from the earliest ages. My recommendation would be to not attempt to reinvent the wheel on this one. There are some amazing resources out there that not only are easy and user friendly, but also have significant content that moves children strategically toward spiritual development.

This is one that took us a while to get a handle on. In the early days (because we knew so little about what we were doing), our philosophy was "*Make 'em smile and give 'em candy when they leave.*" In the recent years, we have connected with North Point's philosophy of child development which, in my opinion, is second to none (www.252basics. com). The key to remember is that even big church resources and curriculums can be adapted down to a small and mobile setting. Don't take no for an answer. Figure out how to make it work. For instance, we have TV's on wheeled carts that can be wheeled in to our classrooms, and our kids love it. It can be done. It will just take some forethought.

When dealing with the kids' environments, nurseries are another essential for reaching and keeping young families. The key here is man power and cleanliness. Don't be surprised if it takes new people some time to trust your nursery department. This is one we had to not let throw us. Couples would bring their babies in the main auditorium for several weeks before they would actually trust us with their kids. We tried to not freak out on them. Rather, we would just gently encourage them to take advantage of our nurseries as God gave us opportunity.

When considering nurseries in a mobile context, one must consider the following. First of all, we have found the big foamy connecting mats are better than carpet because carpet gets grungy and collects a great deal of dirt over a period of time. However, the foam mats can be laid out weekly and then immediately cleaned with a *Swiffer* mop or *Clorox* wipes. Secondly, depending on the room your nurseries are in, you'll also have to consider how you can cover things like soda machines, vending machines, or desk drawers. Little kids are especially known for putting their hands up inside them, etc.

8. Parking Lots

After moving into the school, I took a walk in our parking lot five minutes before service started one Sunday, just to see what it feels like out there when everyone else is already inside. I was amazed at what I felt. It was quiet and big and lonely and uninviting. I immediately took this information back to our team, and we began to strategize about what we could do to make our parking lot feel more like a Next Level environment. It was incongruent with every other environment we were trying to create on Sunday morning.

71

We have since added a speaker with music from the auditorium, more signs, and big banners with the church logo on them at the entrance. We want people to feel like something good is about to happen to them as they pull in the parking lot! It has made a big difference for us. Everything matters. (It's kind of ironic that we have a "parking lot to parking lot" philosophy, but we were forgetting the parking lot.)

Forcing Yourself to See Your Environments Through Fresh Eyes

One of the dangers of doing church weekly is not being able to see things that previously would have stuck out like a sore thumb. The longer you stay at a location, the more strategic you'll have to be at forcing yourself to see things through a new person's eyes. Don't let things get sloppy in any environment. It's always great to have friends from outside your church come in for a Sunday and walk through as if they were brand new and knew nothing and no one. Give them permission to give you honest feed back. Your environments will be better for it, even though it may sting a little at first.

In order to do this effectively, you'll probably have to take off your "this is going to be a lot of work" hat and put on your "this is best for the organization" hat for the sake of the new person. It won't always be worth it, but it will always be worth it.

Understanding the 1 - 2 -3 Principle

We learned there are three slopes that every element of your church can take. Every element of your church is on one of these three slopes all the time. It is either a one, a two, or a three. Being able to identify which slope a particular area is on helps you know what to do with it. Allow me to explain:

72

Slope 1 is a rise. If something is on the first slope, it's helping you build momentum in your church. In other words, it's *raising* your church upward. So, if the quality of your worship is a one, then it's helping you.

Slope 2 is level. When elements reach the second plane, they become neutral. They're neither helping, nor hurting the momentum in your church. For example, in our second year at the movie theater, the signs we were using were small 16 x 20 inch framed signs sitting on black easels. They were full color, but they weren't great. For all intents and purposes, they were a two. They weren't hurting us, but they weren't exactly creating momentum for us either.

Slope 3 is a decline. This is when a particular element of your church moves from being positive or even neutral, to actually harming the momentum of your church. For instance, if no one is in charge of making sure the carpets you use to cover the floors in your nurseries are being cleaned periodically, they'll quickly become a three. Parents of infants will not put their babies in a room with dirty carpets. Consequently, they'll either take their baby into church with them, or they'll leave your church. Either way, it hurts. (Unfortunately, those are the small and virtually invisible things that are deal makers or breakers for many people in your church.)

If you have been doing church for a while, the 1-2-3 Principle can be a filter for every element of your church. Taking two hours with your leadership team and giving every element an honest grade of one, two, or three will help you know the areas that need the most attention immediately.

Another way to review your church is to bring in fresh eyes from the outside. If a friend or relative is coming to visit over a Sunday in the near future, empower him or her to *critique* your environments from parking lot to parking lot. Those insights will be priceless to improving your environments.

Concluding Thoughts on the Parking Lot to Parking Lot Philosophy

Howard Shultz had it right. When it comes to excellence and consistency, everything matters! Developing a "Parking Lot to Parking Lot" Philosophy with your leadership will position you to keep eyes and ears on the little things that make a huge impact on those attending your church.

ONE FINAL SIDENOTE: Never cut corners on quality, especially in areas that directly touch people... kids check-in tags, donut plates, bulletins, and offering envelopes are all areas that directly come in contact with the public. Don't scrimp there. There are a hundred reasons why people won't come back to a church. Don't let something small like a foam plate versus a plastic plate be one of them. Everything matters.

Chapter 4

Questions for the Huddle

Discussion Starters for Teams

1. When was the last time your team experienced a church environment different from your own? Spend some time talking about the various elements you experienced and how they compare to the environments you are trying to create in your church.

2. Are the environments of your church creating the optimum environments for newcomers? Spend some time as a team thinking through every environment of your church and how you can improve it by two levels.

3. What environments of your church are adding momentum, which environments are neutral and which environments are actually working against the momentum of your church?

Chapter 5

Voices on the Field

Up-the-middle churches learn from others

9-12-15

O ne of the most difficult skills a quarterback must learn is the ability to listen to the right voices on the field. If you're a football fan, then you know how loud a football game can be: screaming fans, defensive players yelling out distractions, referees blowing whistles, teammates shouting commands, the loud speaker booming out music. For a quarterback, learning to tune in the right voices and tune out the wrong ones often means the difference between winning and losing.

The same is true for leaders in an up-the-middle church. Voices bombard us from every direction: fans, critics, teammates, friends, family members, coaches, leaders from the past, and the list goes on and on. Learning which voices to tune in and which voices to tune out can be the difference between fumbling the ball or scoring your next touchdown. The distance between winning and losing in an up-the-middle reality is measured by the voices we listen to.

As I mentioned earlier in the book, when we started the church, we knew a lot about what we *didn't* want to be, and very little about what we *did* want to be as a church. Therefore, when we got to Southwest Florida, we began to seek out others who were doing church differently than we had ever seen in the past. Thus began the learning process of voices.

4/12/15

Good point

Hearing Voices Everywhere

There are countless voices that bombard us everyday. Cable TV and the Internet make sure of it. Just spend the evening flipping channels or browsing websites and you'll discover that everybody has something to say, something to sell, and something they want us to hear.

In ministry, the same dynamic exists. There are all kinds of voices that are attempting to input into what we're doing. Learning to filter through voices, tune some in, and turn the volume on others down will be a huge key to bringing focus to your church. The other option is spiritual schizophrenia. Pastors who don't learn to be selective about the voices they allow in send a confusing message to those they lead, and, consequently, create a schizophrenic church unsure of their direction and purpose.

Turning Some Voices Down

Because we desired to create a church like nothing we had ever been exposed to before, we had to start by turning some voices down in our lives. The first voice we had to turn down was the negative or pessimistic voice. There were those in our lives who weren't really in support of what we wanted to do. They had pretty much given us the *"don't call us, we'll call you"* treatment.

The second voice we had to turn down was the skeptical voice. In the early days of the church, there were some people who began attending who were constantly questioning the way things were being done and doubting the vision. The minute we recognized those types of people, we attempted to move their voice further from our ears.

The third voice we had to turn down was the "old way" voice: the voices of those who represent a ministry approach that is no longer

9-12-15

THESE people should NOT BE on the Al TEAM.

relevant to our world today. (I wrestled with the phrase to use on this one. By using the word *old*, I'm not referring to a person's age as much as I am to the mindset they carry. I have met some people who are younger than me but have an *old mindset*.) What I am referring to are leaders who have a pre-conceived belief in the only way that church should be done. Again, please don't hear what I'm not saying. I'm not saying there is anything wrong with that way of doing church. I just know the vision of Next Level Church is centered on a strong conviction that church couldn't look the way church always has *and* be effective in reaching the emerging generation. With that being said, we found ourselves at a place where we needed to turn down those voices.

Changing Radio, Changing Church

To see how culture and the times have changed, one needs to look no further than the evolution of radio. Throughout the twentieth century, AM radio dominated. In fact, I grew up listening to Chicago Cubs games on 720 AM WGN out of Chicago. I can still hear the voice of Harry Carey singing "Take Me Out to the Ballgame" during the seventh inning stretch. Thank God for AM Radio.

FM radio came into its glory in the 70's and 80's and took radio to a whole new level. Stereos and boom boxes took my listening pleasure to a whole new level! I can still remember the name of the two top DJ's on the morning show in our area (Charlie and Tony). They were on 97.3 WMEE. Nice. However great FM Radio was, the world of radio continued to evolve, which brings us to present day.

Today, XM Satellite radio is making its mark on our culture, offering greater choices and quality for a new generation. Most every new car comes with an XM Radio option upon purchase, and I can now listen to every Major League baseball game on XM Radio on demand. It's not just the Cubs anymore; it's all 30 teams. XM Radio has changed the way the world listens.

Just as XM radio brought a whole new approach to radio, the church of the next generation is bringing a whole new approach to church. It is my belief that if we're going to reach the emerging generation, it will probably be a result of creating an XM style of church, rather than an AM style. We had to identify those voices that were immovable in their approach to doing church and begin to marginalize them.

Knowing who to tune out is just as important as knowing who to tune in. I would seriously consider making this whole issue of voices a matter of prayer in the coming weeks. Who are the AM Voices that need to be turned down? And who are the XM Voices that need to be turned up in your world?

Turning Some Voices Up

There are a lot of great voices emerging in the Body of Christ today: Leaders who are doing church effectively, and voices we can learn and glean ideas from. As an up-the-middle leader, it is essential to learn the art of strategically zeroing in on a few voices. My recommendation to any pastor is to find three voices that can bring different perspectives and emphases to the forefront of your mind.

1. Find someone who you want to be like (when you grow up).

For me, it was Andy Stanley. As you're about to hear in the pages of this chapter, when we were opened up to Northpoint's culture, I was personally able to say, "That's what I dream of our church looking, feeling, and being like." I read everything Andy writes and I listen to everything I can get my hands on from Northpoint. I found someone to be like.

Simple church – plant churches!

2. *Find people who are doing what you want to be doing.*

This one has many facets for us as leaders. Questions that were beneficial for me were:

- *"Who do I want to be like in my style of communication?"* Knowing all that I know about my individual gifts and talents as a communicator, who is similar enough that I can begin modeling myself after?

- *"Who do I want to lead like?"* My answer to this one was John Maxwell. I read everything he writes, period. I'm fearful for the pastor who isn't well read in John Maxwell. He's just that solid.

- *"Who is developing the business systems and processes like I want to?"* My mentor in the business, financial, and entrepreneurial thinking category is Robert Kiyosaki. Again, I read everything this guy or his advisors write. Every pastor should read *Before you Quit your Job*. He has such incredible wisdom and insight for church planters and pastors; it's almost scary. All you have to do is change the word *Entrepreneur* to *Pastor,* and the book will come alive.

- *"Who is thinking like I want to be thinking?"* For me, I found this voice in the ARC. The life-giving approach to ministry they have on everything is infectious. When I grow up I want to be as life-giving as they are!

3. *Find someone who is a step or two ahead of you.*

Seek out those who are a step or two ahead of you. Find a couple of pastors who will make themselves available for you to pick their brain three or four times a year. Connect with them on a personal level and watch how they manage their time, staff, personal life, schedule, and priorities. My friend Randy Bezet in Bradenton, FL (www.baysidecommunity.org) calls it having "peers you can do life with." Randy is one of those guys for me. I also have a couple of pastor friends in my city whose churches are about twice our size. I make an effort regularly to schedule a lunch with them.

This will be something that you'll probably have to *make time* to do. It won't just happen by itself. The pace of ministry pushes us toward isolation. And finding guys who are a step or two ahead of you will require humility, patience, and time. But as someone who has worked really hard at this, I can definitely say the time you invest will be worth it.

Amplifying the Voice of Andy Stanley

We were about four months into our church plant, and were sponges for anything we could get our hands on concerning church, leadership, and team development. As a leadership team, we had already worked through a couple of John Maxwell's books on leadership and team building when Dave, one of the guys who moved here with us, came to me and said that he had found a conference in Atlanta that John Maxwell was hosting. It was called *Catalyst.* I can remember being in the early stages of our church and watching every penny, so when I saw the $200 price tag per ticket, I almost choked, but I really felt like we were supposed to be at this conference. So we paid out of pocket for me, my wife, and Dave to go. (I actually think Dave paid for his own ticket. Things were tight.)

The three of us drove up to Atlanta and were exposed for the first time to the ministry of Northpoint Community Church. Needless to say, we were blown away. John Maxwell spoke in the first session and had some great things to say. In the second session, the pastor of Northpoint spoke. His name was Andy Stanley. Oh my gosh! I sat there in the balcony of their church with my jaw on the floor.

When we broke for lunch and were walking to the car, I turned to my wife and Dave and said, "I don't think I've heard anyone so captivating in my entire life." That conference was the day we began amplifying the voice of Andy Stanley. He was able to articulate what

SOR AR 9/2009
1) Simple church Book

we had been feeling in our heart for so long. Next Level Church is what it is today because of the voice of Andy Stanley.

Picking Your Voices Wisely

I want to conclude this chapter on voices by offering the following advice based on what we've learned.

So important

Get out of your own stream. With so little time because of the demands of leading a church, it's tempting to simply look to those mentors and leaders that have been in your life for a long time. That's not necessarily a bad thing. However, there are so many churches out there doing church amazingly well. It just takes a bit of searching on our part to find them.

Ask other guys who they're listening to and watching. One of the questions I love to ask other pastors is "Who are you listening to?" As I mentioned earlier in the book, we resolved on day one to attempt to learn something from everyone. Don't miss that opportunity.

Don't be afraid to get out of your church once in a while. A big mistake pastors make (which we'll talk more about in chapter 12) is to not get away from their church and see other models and ways of doing church. It's refreshing, challenging, and motivating all at the same time.

In closing, I would challenge you to pick your voices wisely. Few other things will influence the DNA of your church, especially when your church is small, like the voices you allow to speak into your life as the leader.

Chapter 5

Questions for the Huddle

Discussion Starters for Teams

1. What voices do you need to turn down as a team?

2. What voices do you need to begin turning up as a team? What books / CD's / DVD's / Conferences can you experience together in an effort to grow and stretch one another?

3. What voices can you begin tuning in that are two steps ahead of you?

Chapter 6

Defining the Touchdowns of Your Church

9-12-15

Up-the-middle churches use core process to grow people

Iremember playing flag football as a kid. There wasn't too much strategy involved (at least, not that I can remember) when it came to running plays and scoring touchdowns. Our coaches (a few guys who had played football in high school) tried hard to put us in the right place on the field and then tell us how to run a play. Unfortunately, things didn't go as well as they would have liked. Most of the time, we ended up handing the ball to the fast kid, letting him try and outrun the other team's fast kid. There was no strategy for actually scoring touchdowns.

Too many churches take a similar approach to assimilating people into the life of the church. There's a lot of motion on the field, but as far as strategy is concerned, there's not much. Up-the-middle churches take a different approach. They take time to define their *touchdowns*, and then they build everything around getting people to that point.

Learning That One Size Does Not Fit All

A Core Process is the term churches use to describe the path they desire for people to take to move from a first time attendee to a fully assimilated member of a church. Though churches vary greatly about how they define someone as being fully assimilated, each church should

84

have a core process in place that moves people to a desired destination of connection to their local church.

When it comes to core process, there are as many models out there as there are churches. One size definitely does not fit all. What works for the big dogs does not automatically translate down to the small or medium-sized church. Leaders of large churches like Rick Warren, Chris Hodges, and Bill Hybels have done a phenomenal job of creating a core process that works for many church contexts.

What is needed in an up-the-middle reality has more to do with customizing your core process to uniquely fit your culture, rather than a cut and paste approach. This can prove to be a lot more of an art than a science.

The question we eventually had to answer was, "*What are we responsible for?*" In this chapter, we will talk through the specific core process of Next Level Church, but let me add a disclaimer right here: It's still a work in progress. Since 2002, we have struggled with successfully locking in our core process. It continues to morph today. In the early days our core process was *Come and come back*. A couple of years in, it transitioned to a rather extensive and detailed system of phone calls, e-mails and follow up that eventually became too cumbersome to continue doing. It has taken several forms until we have arrived at what we have today.

My goal is not to give you the One-Size-Fits-All Core Process Wheel, but rather to get you to think about the path people need to take in order to assimilate into the life of your church.

Understanding Our Responsibility

For too long, churches have owned too much of the responsibility to provide *everything* for everybody. Consequently, church attendees have embraced a *consumer mentality*. Discovering what we're responsible for at each phase of the core process has placed the ownership back on the attendee for his own spiritual growth, nourishment, and health.

I recommend doing three things when thinking through your core process. First, keep it simple. Eliminate as many of the hoops for people to jump through as possible. Second, determine what is most essential for people to know, in order for them to make an educated decision on whether they should make your church their home. Third, make the path from one step to another ridiculously easy, strategic, and obvious.

Our Core Process in a Nut Shell

Our core process has four basic quadrants: visit, attend, serve, and lead. That's it. Nothing fancy. The focus of our core process is on leadership development; therefore, we have designed a systematic way for people to assimilate into the life of the church and ultimately end up in a place where their life is impacting the lives of those around them. We believe this simple four-quadrant process allows our church the environments to build people, but places the ownership on the individual.

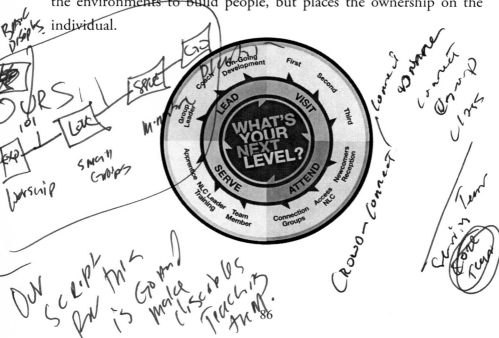

Matt Kelle*

(like

Connect
3rd

The First Quadrant: VISIT

The first quadrant of our core process is *visi* obvious, but we see our Sunday mornings as ou Sunday morning is the entry point for 90% of NL We want people to *visit* three times. We don't underestimate how huge of a deal it is for people to come back. If a person comes once, that means your marketing was successful. If they come back twice, it means that your Sunday morning was successful. Huge difference. Getting people to come back three times is a huge win for us!

Our responsibility during this phase is to provide an opportunity for them to check us out and begin connecting with God. We understand that most NLC attendees have either never been in relationship with God before or have been distant for a very long time. The entire goal of the *visit* quadrant is to create a safe, predictable environment where people can get a feel for who we are, and how we relate to God.

We track our first, second, and third time visitors meticulously. We use three different free gifts located at three individual kiosks in our foyer area. Each week, the gifts keep getting better. Week one is simply an eight minute audio CD explaining who we are as a church and a personal letter from me thanking them for taking time to check out NLC. Week two is a Next Level Church travel coffee mug, and week three is a $10 Starbucks card. Inside the card, we encourage them to take someone to coffee *on us,* and at some point, share why they've come to NLC three times. It's an amazing tool for relational, word-of-mouth marketing to take place.

By the time a person attends Next Level Church three times, we have invested close to $20 in them already. Our thinking behind that is simple: we see it as an investment in them. By adding value to them in a variety of ways, we increase the value of our church in their eyes. We create multiple reminders that can appear throughout their week the travel coffee mug) that reminds them of the great experience they had last weekend at our church.

Here's one additional thought about the amount of money we invest in a visitor's first three visits. The average adult attendee of Next Level Church gives on average $25 per week in the offering. And statistics say that if a person attends a church for more than four times, they have an 85% likelihood of making it their long-term home. That means that by the time a person attends three times, we're only one week away from recouping our initial investment. It's just something to think about.

The Second Quadrant: ATTEND

The transitional statement between the *visit* quadrant and the *attend* quadrant is "Don't just visit, attend." If all someone does is visit, they'll never become all that God wants for them to become. The *attend* quadrant is designed to help people move from visitors to attendees. It consists of three components: our newcomers' reception, Access NLC, and our connection groups.

We do our newcomers' reception once a month on sight immediately following our Sunday morning worship services. We advertise it as *a 10-15 minute reception for anyone who has attended three times*. We communicate it as their opportunity to meet some of the staff, hear more of our heart, and find their next step. At the newcomers' reception, we have a table with snacks and candy, and several bistro tables set up where people can stand and mingle. Some of the staff and a few key leaders are there to introduce themselves and get to know the newcomers. Once everyone is in, we gather their attention and share for about five minutes.

Our Executive Pastor introduces the staff and their spouses and communicates each staff member's area of responsibility. After the introductions, he invites them to Access NLC, which happens the next Sunday evening.

At Access NLC, we communicate three things. First is our story of how we got to Southwest Florida, second are the four quadrants of the core process and third is how they can continue to grow and be a part of what God is doing at NLC. In the early days, we would hold this event everywhere from our home, to a Board of Director's home, to a clubhouse in a community. We now host it in our warehouse space.

The content for this event has morphed a lot since we began in 2002. It started out as a two or three hour time commitment, complete with a lot of doctrine and structural content about the government of our church, our bi-laws, etc. We realized we were providing a lot of information that was interesting, but not essential. The big question we ended up asking was "*What information do people really need / want to know to decide if Next Level Church is the place for them and their family?*" We have streamlined the content down to one hour.

At the end of Access NLC the people are encouraged to do three things: First is fill out a "Regular Attender" card. This provides a place for them to *cross the line* and say NLC is *their* church. Second is to pursue meaningful connections by jumping into a Connection Group. Third is to become a team member, which transitions them into the third quadrant.

One quick sidenote. Over the years, we have struggled with making small groups work. It may be due to any number of factors ranging from recognizing that not everyone could, would, and wanted to be in a traditional small group setting to child care or even geographic location.

There are many small group theories and methods out there that are working successfully, so there is no reason for me to elaborate further on the subject. We currently use a "Free-Market" or "Interest Based" type of small groups, however I know that every up-the-middle church will have to determine the best method for attendees to connect to one another.

In order to do church up-the-middle, there must be a solid system in place to be sure attendees are connecting in meaningful relationships. We wholeheartedly believe that if someone doesn't connect, they will disconnect. The *Attend* quadrant is designed to make sure that doesn't happen.

The Third Quadrant: SERVE

The transitional statement from the *attend* quadrant to the *serve* quadrant is "Don't just attend, serve." We understand that if all people do is visit or attend, they'll never reach their full potential. True spiritual growth begins to happen when we move from a focus on ourselves to a focus on others. That's what the left side of the circle is all about.

The *serve* quadrant consists of three components: Becoming a team member, participating in the NLC three hour leadership training, and becoming an apprentice. As I mentioned a moment ago, at the end of Access NLC, we invite people to become team members. A team member is anyone who serves in any capacity across NLC, from set up and tear down crews, to musicians or kids workers. Team members are the ones who make this organization happen.

The second component is participating in the NLC three hour leadership training. We understand that for our team members to embody the DNA and culture of our church, we must be intentional about communicating what matters most to us as leaders and how we make decisions in relationship to ministering to others. The training gives everyone a baseline on the general leadership principles that lead to thinking like an NLC leader. After someone has become a team member, we encourage them to attend this training session, which happens once a month.

Again, let me state that the way we flesh out our core process continues to morph and change on a consistent basis. We are currently pursuing ways of making our NLC Leader Training more accessible through the internet, etc. The emphasis is not on the "What" or the "How" as much as it is on the "Why" behind it all.

The final component of the *serve* quadrant is becoming an apprentice. After someone has a general knowledge of NLC leadership, his next step is to receive specific training within a department in order to grow in his influence of others. Apprenticeship adds intentionality for every NLC leader to think in terms of sharing with someone else how they think and do the work of the ministry at NLC.

The Fourth Quadrant: LEAD.

The transitional statement from the *serve* quadrant to the *lead* quadrant is "Don't just serve, lead." Our responsibility in the *lead* quadrant is to create an environment for people to step into their destiny and truly become everything God wants for them to be. There are three components of the *lead* quadrant: Being a group leader, becoming a coach, and continuing with on-going development.

We define a group leader as anyone who leads a group of any kind. It could be a small group in their home, a ministry team, or even a kids' small group. The goal is for people to see their responsibility in adding intentionality to that which they're already doing. Wherever they are serving, according to their passions, we want to give them permission to be intentional about influencing and leading others.

Coaches are those who are capable of leading leaders. Coaches are high capacity leaders who often drive entire departments within departments of NLC. Coaches are responsible for mentoring apprentices and motivating team members to continue to step up and see themselves in a greater way.

The on-going development component is geared toward creating a consistent opportunity for NLC leaders to hear the heart and philosophy of our church in repeated fashion. We do this through an every other month *all-leader meeting* that takes place on Sunday afternoon after church from 1 to 2:30 pm. This meeting is centered around celebrating the stories of life-change together, casting vision and keeping everyone on the same page. This bi-monthly meeting also gives us an opportunity to teach leadership principles that keep everyone growing together as a team. Leaders are also encouraged to create a personal growth track for themselves, as well. Adding Intentionality to leadership equals growth, and we want to see people growing in their relationship to God and others. That's the focus of core process.

Concluding Thoughts on Core Process

There are as many core processes out there as there are churches. As an up-the-middle church, you don't have the luxury of not having a strategy for scoring touchdowns with your people. Developing a core process can help you do that. It doesn't have to be complicated to be effective but once you have defined your core process, don't get distracted from it. Don't feel pressured to add all sorts of sub-ministries just because another church has them or people put pressure on you.

Two final thoughts on Core Process: First, keep it simple at first. Rome wasn't built **Once you have defined it, exploit it!** Do everything you can to make sure that every person knows exactly where they are in the process and what their next step needs to be. I believe that pastors can't hit this enough. If we really believe our core process leads to

life-change, then how can we not exploit it? Your core process is the
touchdown of your church!

Our
process
is how will we
help people
Follow Jesus
as they choose

1(celebrate
+
challenge ''

celebrate
where they
are and
challenge
to grow.

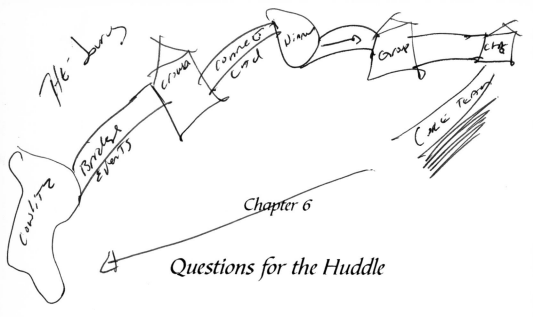

Chapter 6

Questions for the Huddle

Discussion Starters for Teams

1. What is the Core Process of your church? Spend some time as a team discussing how a person moves from first time attendee to a fully assimilated member in your church.

2. How streamlined is the Core Process of your church? Are there any unnecessary or cumbersome steps?

3. How well do the people of your church understand the Core Process of your church? Spend some time as a team discussing how to exploit your Core Process throughout your church.

Chapter 7

Creating Home-Field Advantage

Up-the-middle churches think differently about facility

I love watching the last few weeks of the NFL season each year. There are always several teams on the bubble, teetering between playoff hopes and elimination. But for the teams at the top of each division, their motivation in the last few weeks of the regular season centers around one thing: home-field advantage. Having home-field advantage is everything. It's the difference between 75,000 fans screaming during your set of downs or your opponent's set of downs. It's the difference between familiar and foreign.

The facility reality in the church world today is changing. No longer is facility the focal point of ministries. As the millennial generation emerges in the church-world, focus on facility will continue to diminish. The pragmatism and focus on serving in the young generation is pushing the desire and need for extravagant and excessive facilities to the way side.

Another reason permanent facilities are taking a lesser role in the church world today is because of the cost involved. Rising land and construction costs make the reality of an all-encompassing, everything included, one-stop-shop church building less of a reality for a lot of churches today. As the new normal, up-the-middle churches are being forced to think differently about facility.

Rethinking Facility

The up-the-middle church is one that is willing to rethink facility. Asking questions like:

- "What if our facility didn't have to look like it has looked in the past?"
- "What if we could produce the same end result of life-change for a fraction of the cost?"
- "What if there is more than one way to think of facility today?"
- "What if we could leverage worldly facilities for Kingdom purposes?"
- "What if stewardship of resources could be allocated to *people* ministry rather than *building* maintenance?"

Having a *one-stop-shop* facility is not a bad thing. In fact, just as I've said in previous chapters, we need all kinds of churches with all kinds of facilities. My children attend a Christian school that is housed inside of a *one-stop-shop* church that is having a huge impact on our community. Other churches in our community have very limited and specific worship space. Still, others are being effective in a mobile reality. My goal is to challenge you, the up-the-middle leader, to think differently about the reality of your facility.

Since we began Next Level Church in 2002, we have taken a different approach to the way we promote, communicate, and cast vision for the facility component of our church. The result has been amazing. Now, several years later, we have a church full of people who see facility differently. Even those who have come from a more traditional church background are thinking differently about the facility component of a local church.

Often, permanent facility can be seen as an excuse, or a limitation to ministry. Occasionally, it can even become an idol. Many churches use the lack of a permanent facility as an excuse. They say things like, *"When we have a building, then we'll..."* Those are limiting thoughts, and great churches don't get built by leaders with limiting thoughts. Great churches find a way to go up-the-middle and succeed, regardless of facility limitations. When Rick Warren started Saddleback church in southern California, they met in dozens of different locations in the first few years of their existence. They didn't let facility dictate what they could or couldn't do.

When a church's focus moves from building people to building buildings, its effectiveness begins to diminish. The unbelieving world around us is weary of churches whose entire focus is on buildings and fundraising. I believe the church of the future will be less facility-focused than ever before. The new normal concerning facility will see buildings as a tool to build people and not the other way around.

Understanding That Mobile Doesn't Have to Mean Less

More and more up-the-middle churches today are leveraging the mobile reality for their weekend gatherings and they're having tremendous success! From high schools and middle schools to community centers and movie theaters, the mobile reality is a picture of the future of the up-the-middle church. In fact, our church has used the mobile reality to have a great impact on the region of Southwest Florida. We would not be the church we are today if it weren't for the opportunity that a mobile reality provided for us.

I always cringe when I read the website of a church who is mobile and they insinuate their location is *temporary*. Here's why. We do a disservice to our people when we lead them to believe they are somehow *less of a church*, or *not there yet* because they don't own the building they worship in. Up-the-middle churches do whatever it takes to make facility work for them, and not the other way around.

The other disservice we do to our people by communicating a *temporary* philosophy is that we're not happy or content with the present location God has given us. We miss a valuable opportunity to teach our people to be thankful right where they are. After all, God has provided a school or theater or meeting space. Getting our eyes so focused on *someday and when…* forfeits the praise God deserves *today and now.*

If people believe that a mobile church is not quite as good as a non-mobile church, they will be less likely to invite their un-churched friends. Not creating a culture of gratitude for the mobile facility God has given you also makes people question their decision to be apart of your church. My children have never known church as anything other than portable. Since they were able to walk, we have allowed our two boys the privilege of being apart of the set up and tear down teams. (There's nothing cuter than two little boys walking around picking up door stops after church!)

The bottom line is that people will define *normal* by what you lead them to believe it is supposed to be. Up-the-middle leaders create a home field advantage by defining *normal* as wherever God has provided for you to meet.

Making Your Facility Work for You, Not the Other Way Around

When we were doing church in the movie theater, people would often ask us, "What are you thinking concerning a building?" Our response was simply, "As long as the movie theater works for us, we'll stay here. But the minute we feel like we're working to make it work, then we'll start looking somewhere else." And that's exactly what happened.

On Father's Day weekend, 2005, my friend Randy Bezet, who pastors an ARC church in Sarasota, came down for the weekend.

Randy and his wife, Amy represented a fresh set of eyes on everything we were doing.

After spending a Sunday with us in the movie theater, Randy and Amy shared with us how limited they thought we were in the theater. They could see we were working to make it work, rather than it working for us. They challenged us to start praying and believing for God to show us what our next step could look like. It took six months for us to secure South Fort Myers High School, and it was no easy task. Because the school was brand new, the auditorium wasn't even finished yet. In addition, there were many other churches that wanted the space. By God's grace, we ended up there, and it was a perfect next step.

Since moving into South Fort Myers High School in the spring of 2006, the facility question went away. I would venture to say the vast majority of people who attend Next Level Church on a Sunday morning forget they are in a mobile church. Our set up crews do a phenomenal job of converting the space to a Next Level *feel*. *Consequently,* we see it as a long-term option for us. But if I'm being honest, I have to admit, it does take a lot of work. Making a mobile reality feel like a home-field advantage requires intentionality, determination, and commitment.

Seeing Mobile Church as Who You Are

The most important piece of advice I can give you about doing mobile church is to **make it what you're doing!** We often have people who say to us, "*It just looks like a lot of work!*" And in reality, it is. But mobile church is our reality, and we embrace it wholeheartedly. What other choice do we have? Our church people don't think anything about it anymore. They love the environments we create, and that makes it all worth it. As long as we're able to create those environments with excellence, mobile church is an amazing way to keep overhead low, and have a first-class facility.

Because more and more churches are mobile, it's important to do some homework on how to make mobile church a part of your culture. Mobile church can't be something you do. It must become apart of who you are. If churches don't cross that bridge, they'll end up burning out. So, in essence, the most important thing you can do first as a leader is embrace your mobility. Your primary job is to cast a vision for it. You can never over-communicate to your set up and tear down crews how what they do fits into the big vision of your church. Share stories with them of lives that were changed in an environment they helped create. Make sure they understand how setting up a chair or emptying a trash can have eternal value tied to it.

Next, you must create an identity around your mobile church. Make it the *in* thing. It is what you're doing, so build an identity around it. Make it its own deal. Get t-shirts or hats. Give your set up and tear down crews a name.

Once you have created the identity, it is time to figure out how to schedule workers. The set up and tear down crews of your church will probably be two of the biggest ministries you have. Don't approach them haphazardly. Treat them with respect and help people to avoid burn-out.

Finally, if you're going to embrace your mobile reality, you've got to celebrate your volunteer teams. Bring them coffee and donuts, or have someone cook them a steak and eggs breakfast one Sunday morning. Buy them gift cards. Know when their birthdays are and do something nice for them. The set up and tear down teams will make or break your church in many ways. If you are able to keep people motivated week in and week out, gaining yardage up-the-middle will be exponentially easier.

Getting Systematized in Your Set Up and Tear Down

Creating systems and schedules for set up and tear down will be huge. This can be difficult because, in addition to actually doing the work of set up and tear down, your leaders will also feel the burden of teaching and training others. Teaching others the "Why" behind the "What" and "How" will yield huge benefits in a few months. The eventual goal is for your key leaders (staff) to simply become cheerleaders and trouble shooters. It doesn't mean they won't be doing any of the heavy lifting any longer; it simply means their primary role in set up and tear down will be oversight and management by walking around rather than being heavily engrossed in the actual labor of it.

Expect the unexpected. Inevitably, things will go wrong or be out of place from week to week. Build extra time into your set up reality for unexpected trouble. If you prepare for it, and expect it each week, it won't throw you as much when it happens. Having extra time makes a mobile world a better place.

Protecting Your Key Leader in Set Up

The sooner you can get your lead pastor out of the set up reality, the better. There is no greater burden on Sunday morning than preaching and communicating the Word. In the early days of our church, when I had to be heavily involved in set up, it was really, really hard. I was trying to carry the burden of the Word, and instead, I found myself losing my cool over little things! There were many Sundays in the movie theater days when my associate, Mike, would pull me aside and say, "Get out of here, dude. Get alone, pray and settle down." It's hard. The sooner you can protect your lead pastor, the better.

Appointing a Point Person

It is so important to make someone on your leadership team or staff the COO or Chief Operations Officer of your Sunday morning set up. This person is ultimately in charge and responsible for every environment you create. This person should not be the lead pastor. If something goes wrong or is missing, people know to contact this person, not the lead pastor. This person should also available to each of the area captains of the individual environments like auditorium, kids, foyer, etc. to assist them and make sure they have everything they need to keep on schedule for your set up timelines.

Concluding Thoughts on Creating Home-Field Advantage

Whether it's a mobile reality or a permanent one, the up-the-middle church knows how to think differently about facility. Is your thinking about facility filtered through a narrow lens? If so, then perhaps you need to begin praying about the issue. Maybe you need to spend an hour with your team dialoguing about new approaches to the facility issue. Or perhaps you need to study other churches who are taking a different approach to facility with an open mind. The new normal in the church world will see facility as a tool to build people and not the other way around.

Chapter 7

Questions for the Huddle

Discussion Starters for Teams

1. What perception have you given to your people about your church facility? Spend some time as a team talking about how you communicate the appropriate message to your church.

2. If you are in a mobile environment, spend some time discussing how you keep your team from experiencing mobile fatigue.

3. How do you need to think differently about your present and future facility needs? Spend some time as a team thinking outside of the box in terms of your facility.

Section 3

The People Side of the Up-the-Middle Church

"...There are no problems we can't solve together, and very few that we can solve by ourselves."

- L.B. Johnson

One of the greatest joys of leading an up-the-middle church is seeing the leaders around our organization soaring higher than they ever thought possible. There's just nothing better! That's what Section 3 is all about!

Finding the Team Captains

Up-the-middle churches discover and empower leaders on the field

9-12

W hen it comes to church, the million-dollar question always revolves around leadership. This is unquestionably one of the largest issues that up-the-middle churches face today. Where do leaders come from? How do you know who to trust? What filter do you use to screen them? How do you develop them? The next two chapters are dedicated to up-the-middle leadership.

The Next Level Church leadership team has morphed a lot since 2002. We have definitely experienced a lot of highs *and* lows in the team building process. From the beginning, my wife and I have had in our heart to build leaders around us. However, I think I underestimated how difficult it would be to manage all of the highs and lows of team life and leadership development.

What started out as six of us sitting around my kitchen table every Sunday night with no paychecks has now morphed into offices full of paid staff and another half dozen or so that function as unpaid staff around us. We have hired, fired, employed, deployed, removed, and accepted resignations over the years. Doing church as a team is never easy, but I wouldn't want to do it any other way.

In the beginning, we experienced the definite frustration I'm sure many up-the-middle leaders feel when the dream is bigger, broader, and more developed than the team. It's definitely a "Whosoever will" mentality. The qualifications are:

1) They must be breathing
2) They must be willing to work hard
3) They must be saved (optional)

That may work initially; however, as a church grows, the requirements grow with it. When a church is smaller or younger, you can get away with raw, inexperienced talent and make more mistakes. But as a church grows in size and maturity, the first place to feel it is in the team. Up-the-middle churches must be prepared for that pressure.

I would definitely say the whole team dynamics thing took me by surprise. I continue to marvel at the time and energy I expend weekly on team interactions, personality conflicts, and leadership development. If you're just starting out and feel like you have more dream than team, don't worry. If you've been going a while and find yourself frustrated at team life, rest assured. God is faithful to bring in the leaders you need at just the right time for the right season. And if you're praying about planting, begin praying now for the team that God wants to be with you as you begin this journey.

Understanding Our Personal Philosophy of Leadership

I am a big believer in people. I believe that vision is probably my primary spiritual gift. I love to look at what *could be* in people and call them up to it! Max DuPree said that, "A leader's primary responsibility is to create reality for people." I think most people, especially twenty and thirty "something's" are looking for someone who will believe in them.

Our leadership structure at NLC reflects that kind of belief in people to a large degree. I guess it's fair to say that I would rather put players on the field knowing they're going to fumble the ball now and then, rather than have them sit on the sidelines just watching.

Implementing Two Baseball Analogies That Have Served Us Well

In spite of writing a football themed book, I happen to be a huge baseball fan. It's my first love! That being the case, baseball analogies tend to make it into my teaching from time to time. Forgive me for straying from football for a moment, but there are two analogies you just have to get.

Analogy #1: Textbook vs. On-the-Field Training

When it comes to the up-the-middle church, there are really only two perspectives on leadership development. They are best seen through a story of my two sons...

I'm teaching my two sons the game of baseball. They both seem interested in the game, and I certainly enjoy putting on my ball glove after dinner. When it comes to teaching my kids the game of baseball, I have two choices. One is to go to Barnes and Noble, pick up a few good books on the rules of baseball, the fundamentals of the game, and the strategy of the game, then proceed to sit them down each night for an hour and teach them the nuances of the game.

The other option is to get them each a glove and a ball, take them out to the yard, and begin in small ways to show them how to throw, catch, and hit. After a few days, we might put out some bases, and begin teaching them some other things like how many balls and strikes a batter gets, and how many outs are in each inning. After that, I would begin to teach them some basic strategy like tagging up on a high fly, or taking a pitch.

The first method certainly presents itself as a more thorough approach to adequately teaching the game of baseball, I suppose. However, the second approach will give my boys a more hands on perspective of what the game is all about. Will some fly balls get dropped in the process of learning the game? Sure, but those moments provide me, as dad and coach, a great place to teach them, stretch their thinking, and coach them on how to handle that situation in the future.

As a church, we have decided we're going to be a place where we put players on the field and coach them along the way. We understand there will be some fly balls that get dropped, but that's a risk we're willing to take so people can begin participating in the game as soon as possible. Having relationships with the players on the field becomes huge in our model of leadership. We understand that in the context of relationship we have the ability to speak into people's lives.

Analogy #2: *The Major League Baseball Farm System*

The developmental system for major league baseball has also been a great analogy for our leadership team. In baseball, there are basically five levels every major league team has in place. The Rookie League, Single A, Double A, Triple A, and the Majors. There are several dynamics that begin to change as a player moves through the developmental leagues of baseball: The stadium size changes, popularity of the team in the city, price of tickets, price of concessions, size of the fan base, skill level of your opponents and skill level of your teammates.

From the early days of our church, it has been great to have an illustration that we can compare ourselves to. We definitely started at the rookie level. We were pretty clueless as to how to even play the game of church. We had very young players on our team who needed a lot of developing and work, and our attendance was pretty small. Some churches are blessed to launch at a higher level. Perhaps their players are more experienced and have more people who are willing to pay a higher ticket price. But that's not our story. We were definitely in the Rookie League for the first nine months of our church. Every Sunday for the first nine months I would come to the theater and think to myself, "this is the day that no one is going to come..." It was a hard time being in the rookie leagues.

Our next step was Single A. I would say right about the time we hit 100 people in Sunday morning attendance, we felt things begin to change in our approach to church and team. The stakes definitely increased a bit. For the first time, we finally felt like we were going to survive and maybe win a game. I actually stopped feeling like nobody was going to show up and started playing for the win.

I would say that the 200 or 250 mark represented the move to Double A in our minds. We were doing two services, actually paying a few people as paid staff, beginning to think bigger thoughts, and our leaders were beginning to envision the future of what this thing could be.

It wasn't until the fall of 2006, after four years, that we broke 400 consistently and began to feel like we were about to move into a Triple A existence. It's the strangest thing to feel the tension of the next level coming upon you. As a leader, you begin evaluating everything, especially your team. You begin asking questions like *"Can this player play at the next level?" "Are they growing at the same pace as the church?" "Are they capable of playing in a bigger stadium, in front of more people, who are paying higher ticket prices?"*

This baseball terminology has given our team a great way to view their personal growth, the growth of our church, and where we're heading: more seats, higher ticket prices, more costly concessions, more publicity, more at stake, TV cameras present, etc. The final major move from Triple A to the "big leagues" happens somewhere near the 1,000 mark in weekend attendance. At the 1,000 mark you can actually pay people to oversee teams who manage the systems of the organization. At that point, you're playing at a whole new level.

I will admit the illustration breaks down a bit in that teams don't change their status, but churches do. In other words, a Double A team in a city is never going to become a Triple A team because in baseball, just the players move up. However, in the church world, players *and* teams move up. Therefore, when it comes to the team, the stakes are even higher. Because if you're team isn't growing at the same pace as the organization, they'll begin to fall behind and hurt the organization. So when the team reaches the point of moving up to a new level, those players who aren't ready will have to be traded, developed, benched, or changed in their position. We have definitely had our fair share of trading, developing, and repositioning of players over the years. Not everyone has stayed with us. In fact, it seems that every time the church was getting ready to move up to the next level, we transitioned players on our team.

John Maxwell says that, "Not everyone is meant to take the entire journey with you." I have lived that quote several times as we have went through the painstaking process of transitioning a teammate. It hasn't always been easy, but I have absolutely marveled at God's faithfulness to move players before we had to. We learned to trust Him completely in those moments. Although the natural tendency is to run to thoughts of "What are we going to do without them?" we have seen God come through every time.

Chapter 8

Questions for the Huddle

Discussion Starters for Teams

1. What is the philosophy of leadership development for your church? Spend some time as a team discussing what the leadership development process of your church looks like.

2. What are the hoops required for leaders to get involved in your church? Spend some time as a team talking through which "hoops" are truly necessary and which could be tweaked or eliminated in order to make leadership development more effective.

3. Are all of the leaders in your organization playing at the level they need to be in order for your church to grow to the next level? Spend some time discussing how you give those leaders every chance to succeed and grow.

Chapter 9

Qualities of Up-the-Middle Teammates

Up-the-middle churches look for distinct attributes in their teams

Even with all of the drama and headaches that teams bring with them, the truth is, when you're talking about doing church up-the-middle, there's really only one option—do it with a team, or don't do it at all. Going up-the-middle is a lonely place, and without the presence of a team, it quickly becomes a virtual desert. The next few pages zero in on six qualities every up-the-middle teammate must embody.

Why These Qualities are Essential

Having quality teammates is crucial for any church. It is imperative to understand the importance and benefits of having a great team. First of all, it can multiply a leader's capacity. Having a team gives you, the leader, the ability to multiply your efforts and effectiveness immediately. Teams provide many eyes, heads, hands and hearts. As you know, in an up-the-middle reality, it's all about creating something from nothing. With that being said, having as many eyes and heads surveying and analyzing a particular scenario or situation becomes priceless. Being able to bounce ideas off of others who understand the vision and goals of your church brings exponential results to your decision making.

From facility decisions, to music style, to length of service and service times, extra eyes and heads are everything. There have been

112

times where our church has approached a scenario and for whatever reason, I can't see the right decision emerging. The minute I invite other team members in on the situation, the answer or wise choice begins to emerge. In fact, the longer we do church as a team, the more dependent I have become on the team to help me make decisions. My team can always see things I can't.

The second benefit of a quality team is the presence of many hands. When it comes to the up-the-middle church reality, it really is true that many hands make light work, or at least lighter work. Creating something from nothing always requires physical energy and effort. Having a great team around you will lighten the physical work load considerably.

In the early days of our church, we didn't even have enough money to buy a trailer for our equipment. We had to store it all in my garage. Because of that, every Saturday night, the six people on our church planting team would drive to our house, which was twenty-five minutes from where they all lived. We would open the garage door and load up all of our equipment into six cars. We knew exactly how it went in and where it fit perfectly! Then on Sunday morning, we would drive to the movie theater and unload all six cars, set up church, do church, tear it all down, load it all back into our six cars, and bring it back to my garage on Sunday evenings before our team meetings. It was a lot of work. And I'm glad we had many hands in those days!

A third benefit of quality teammates is in the idea of many hearts. A team gives you the ability to multiply your heart exponentially. The sooner your team can grab a hold of the vision of what it is you're trying to create, the sooner they can begin to make decisions for you and on your behalf. I recently spend a weekend with an up-the-middle pastor, and I gave him the following recommendation: *"Don't grow a church; grow your team."* If you can grow your team, they'll grow your

113

church! It's so refreshing to know that the burden of carrying the heart of the organization isn't solely on your shoulders.

However, just having a lot of heads, hands, and even hearts doesn't necessarily make a great team. When it comes to the up-the-middle church reality, a question worth addressing is "What qualities should I be looking for in potential team members?" We look for six key areas as a starting point for up-the-middle leaders:

1. Teachability

The #1 quality I have learned to look for in a potential team member is teachability. In my opinion, the importance of this quality is unrivaled. As I mentioned earlier in the book, one of the great benefits we have discovered in an up-the-middle reality is the fact that we learn something from everyone. We believe there are other churches out there doing church way better than we are, and we want to put ourselves around them as frequently as we can; therefore, we become sponges to fresh ideas in the way church is done. We want to live a life of teachability.

Developing the ability to absorb as much information as possible from as many sources as possible is an essential quality for up-the-middle teammates. The idea of teachability begins with the lead pastor and flows down into the rest of the organization. This means developing the skill of listening and being willing to relearn those elements of ministry we think we already know. Our Executive Pastor, Scott Drummond, defines teachability as *"the willingness to relearn that which you think you already know."*

I have the privilege of meeting a number of church planters and pastors every year, and I am always blown away at how many of them miss out on tremendous opportunities to learn simply because they neglect to listen. I understand that God has given them a big vision, and that they've learned a lot; but the up-the-middle reality is like no other ministry endeavor on the planet. So regardless of how much experience one has in church work, believe me, doing church up-the-middle is like nothing they've ever experienced before. And taking a posture of teachability will shorten the growth curve considerably.

I recently met with one church planter who was bursting with potential and energy. He was so excited about the vision God had placed in his heart for his city that it kind of started getting over the top. I sat there thinking, "I know you have a huge vision and are believing God will do great things, but you might actually learn something you don't know if you listen for one minute!" I never want to miss an opportunity to learn something from someone who has been or is where I'm going. There is a big difference between reading the ingredients off the back of a Snicker's bar and actually eating one. You may know a ton about ministry and the vision God has given you, but be careful not to miss out on a chance to glean from someone who has actually done it. → GREAT!

Unfortunately, in an effort to be validated, too many pastors have such a desire to be heard and to share their vision with other; they fail to listen long enough to actually learn anything. Don't make that mistake, no matter what stage your church is in. When you have the privilege of being given time with another pastor who is further along than you, do more listening than talking. Keep deflecting the conversation back to them and their reality. Spend twice as much time preparing for that meeting as you will actually have in the meeting. Come with more questions than you know you'll have time for. Oh yeah, and make sure you have something to write with. Seize every moment with a more experienced leader. There will be time to share your vision, and your gift will make room for itself. The more important factor is to get out of the way of yourself so that your church can actually benefit.

So True! I've Been there

So Good!

As for potential team members, the same fundamental principle applies. You don't want people on your team who think they already know it all. Yes, you want people who are going to bring experience and ideas to the table, but you also want people who are willing to learn from you and from others. That's Teachability.

2. *Adaptability / Flexibility*

Another important quality for potential team members is flexibility. The essence of an up-the-middle church is change. With every step, beginning with creating something from nothing the reality we live in is all about change. You do not need people on your team who are stuck in a certain mindset or way of thinking about how church can and should be done. Placing someone on your team that has trouble seeing beyond a pre-determined way of doing church will be trouble down the road. You want people around you who will keep asking the question, "How could we do this like it's never been done before?"

In an up-the-middle reality, you need people who know how to shift on the fly. Thinking on your feet while running is essential to your ministry context. As a church planter, one benefit we did have was a clean slate. In other words, there were no pre-conceived ways of doing things. At every turn, you are making it up and needing to shift on the fly.

Each week at Next Level Church, we come into Sunday with the assumption that something *will* go wrong. A tire will be flat on a trailer, a microphone won't work right, or something will be missing in some department. In those moments, having people on the team who have the ability to adapt and make it up as they go is priceless. (It will also help to have a tape measure and power drill somewhere close by each week, as well. Trust me, you'll need them more often than you think!) Teammates who know how to be flexible in the midst of a stressful situation are essential.

3. *Positive Attitude*

Another huge component for teammates is the ability to be positive. This may sound trite, basic, or even a given. But the truth is, people with a propensity toward being negative often drift toward new or smaller churches. Why? Because existing churches or larger churches with existing leaders and structures tend to isolate and eliminate negative voices almost instinctively. Most assuredly, in an up-the-middle reality, you will face negative people.

The best way for me to describe what I'm looking for in a team member is in the question "How can it be done?" Too many people have an attitude that often says "It can't be done." At that point, their mind shuts down and they give up. However, positive people tend to drift toward the question "***How*** can it be done?" That question gives our mind the ability to keep thinking about possible solutions.

I often tell our church and our team the following phrase: "We figure it out, we make it up as we go, and we don't take no for an answer because we're church planters. That's what we do." (That will probably be on my tombstone someday, if my team has anything to do with it.) Don't tell me it can't be done; bring me solutions. I've found that more gets done that way! After all, we moved 1,300 miles away from the only home we had ever known to start a church with little money and little help. Don't tell me it can't be done! With God's help and leading, we can do it! We just have to give ourselves permission to do so. Surround yourself with others who believe it too.

4. A Good Work Ethic

You are going to want team members who are willing to work hard—plain and simple. In an up-the-middle reality, there is a lot going on, a limited time to get it done, and limited dollars to fund it. You need people who will put in extra time and energy above and beyond the call of duty. Obviously, that means some people won't be able to make the commitment to join you on your team. That's okay. God's got just the right people to take this journey with you.

Being a part of an up-the-middle church is a long road lined with obscurity in many ways. And when the church is small, the sacrifice can feel far greater than the reward at times. You want people who can see with spiritual eyes the lives that are being touched and changed for eternity's sake. People with a good work ethic know how to get the job done, whether the rewards are visible or not. This type of person is invaluable to your team.

5. Humility

In an up-the-middle reality, there is no room for a leader who is arrogant or self-serving. Let's face it, the road is too long and the journey is too hard to have people on our team who are more interested in advancing their own agenda than the vision of our church. Humility is a key character trait every up-the-middle leader should possess.

In my mind, humility and a lack of confidence are two different things. You need leaders who have a keen understanding of their skill sets and abilities, yet don't use those abilities for personal gain. Humble leaders know how to use their God-given abilities to advance the vision of the organization above any other initiative.

In an up-the-middle reality, there will be people who emerge who are hungry for a title or position within your church. Chris Hodges of the ARC has the following advice for church planters and pastors: "Don't give anybody a title until you're completely sure their heart and motives are in the right place." I love that. The best way to know if someone is deserving of a title in the future is their ability to work without one in the present.

At NLC, we move very slowly in giving out titles. We've created a culture in our church where titles don't mean much. In fact, very few people actually have them at all, and the ones who do have a title never use it to their advantage. Humble leaders go a lot further in an up-the-middle reality than leaders who are title-hungry or position-focused. Humility must be a defining characteristic for leaders on your team.

6. Creativity

A final quality that is essential in an up-the-middle ministry team is creativity. Surrounding yourself with people who will push you creatively is tough but rewarding. I learned early on that I didn't want to be the guy at the table with the best answer. If I'm responsible for always having the best answer, then we're in trouble, because I'm just not that good! (Not to mention the loss of sleep because of the pressure that puts on you.) However, if I can get people around me who are smarter, wittier, and more creative than I am, then all I have to do is create an atmosphere where the best idea wins, *period*.

On a creative level, I think in terms of a beach ball. My job is to bring a beach ball idea to the table and throw it up into the air. The goal is for the team to bat it around and make it better. My primary responsibility then is to make sure it doesn't head in a direction we don't want to go, and to keep it from hitting the floor. The higher the ball goes and the more people that touch it, the better the idea will be in the end. After a creative meeting, I'll go back and process through all that was said and done and determine the fine tuning of the idea.

Creative teammates make us better than we could ever be by ourselves. Keeping things fresh in an up-the-middle reality is tough, and creative teammates make that pursuit much easier.

Concluding Thoughts on the Qualities of Up-the-Middle Teammates

Having the right people on the team is essential if your church is going to become everything that God wants it to be. Dream teams don't happen overnight, but they can happen. As the leader of an up-the-middle church, you must stay committed to the task of developing and building the dream team of your organization. This won't always be easy, but it will always be worth it.

Chapter 9

Questions for the Huddle

Discussion Starters for Teams

1. If someone came in from the outside and observed, what would they say are the top six characteristics of your leadership team? Are they the qualities you desire in the top leaders of your church? Spend some time as a team discussing the top six leadership qualities you collectively desire for your leaders to possess.

2. Because Teachability is one of the most important characteristics of up-the-middle leaders, spend some time talking through the Teachability of each leader.

3. What can you do to develop a strategic growth plan for the areas where each leader in your church is weak? Spend some time as a time discussing tools, resources and books that would help each of you develop your areas of weakness.

Chapter 10

gris

Growing Future Superstars

Up-the-middle churches see their church as a breeding ground for young leaders

One of the great opportunities of an up-the-middle church is the ability to discover, develop, and release young leaders. The up-the-middle environment is a great one for young leaders to grow, develop and thrive. My heart is for young leaders. I believe the church of today and the future will be determined solely based upon the impact that you and I have on the young leaders of today. Let's talk about that for a minute.

One of the greatest blessings in my life is the amazingly talented young leaders in the church. They bring a life and vitality to our church that I could never produce on my own. Even though they make mistakes and lack experience, the benefits they bring to our church far outweigh any headaches or pains they may cause. (Until recently, I was the oldest guy on our team. And believe me, they let me know that I was the oldest.)

The up-the-middle church attracts young leaders for a number of reasons. First, young leaders are attracted to the freedom that exists in a smaller or start up reality. They are drawn to the lack of hoops required to be involved. Second, young leaders like the freshness of an up-the-middle church. They dig that it's not their mom's and dad's church. Third, they're looking for a place to spread their wings. Finally, and perhaps most importantly, they're looking for a spiritual father or mother who has the time to mentor them and believe in them.

That being the case, you will most likely have some tremendous young talent emerge around your church. Here are my most current thoughts on developing young leaders in an up-the-middle church:

1. Don't just work—play.

The young leaders around you want to be a part of your life. They want to see that being in the ministry still means that you're real. They are longing to know you don't live in a plastic house with a plastic family. They want to know that you actually enjoy doing real stuff, just like they do. They want to know that if they follow in your footsteps, they won't have to lose themselves in the process.

Let them see your realness, and if you're worried about the whole submission and authority thing, don't worry. Most young leaders have the ability to know when it's time to work and time to play, and if they don't, it will be a great opportunity to teach them. After all, that's why they're here, right?

2. Don't just work together—learn together.

Take advantage of the opportunity you have to learn with your young leaders. I spend a large percentage of my week meeting one on one with many young leaders. (I estimate that 15% of my work hours each week are spent with young leaders, both on my team and volunteer.) I love seeing potential in someone and giving them a chance to learn and grow. I'm always amazed at how they rise to the level of expectation placed upon them.

One way I have found to develop and teach young leaders is by going through books together. This has proved to be a great way for them to learn how I think about leadership and ministry. Each week we'll read a chapter or two and then discuss it at the beginning of our time together. It's always cool to see that by the end of the book, we're underlining the same things in the chapters. This let's me know that they are beginning to think like I think about leadership, which is the goal.

Be strategic about putting your young leaders in scenarios that will stretch and challenge them to accomplish things they didn't know they were capable of. Coaching and monitoring is huge here. Don't just let them hang out in left field all by themselves. Work with them so they'll know how you think about certain scenarios and issues, which leads us to the third point.

3. Don't just work—explain the work.

Young leaders need to know how you think about what you're doing. As I mentioned earlier in the book, I call it *having the conversation*. Don't be afraid to assume they know nothing, even though you know they know something. I will often have the conversation with a staff person as a reference point for future conversations. Having the conversation provides an opportunity to teach them how I think and why I do what I do the way I do it. It also gives them permission to get inside my head. If they can think like you think, they'll lead like you lead.

There are always three components to our ministries: The What, the How, and the Why. Too often we rush to the What and the How. After all, this is where the work gets done, right? However, the DNA transfer of the culture happens when we take the time to unpack the Why behind the What and the How. It usually takes a short amount of time to explain the Why behind the What and How, but it always yields huge dividends in leadership development. We must not assume the leaders around us know Why we do what we do in our churches.

Explaining the Why behind the work of the ministry strengthens the young leaders around you.

wow!

4. Don't just work—let them in your head.

There is a philosophy of ministry that emerged two generations ago that leadership should be guarded and private. That we should keep people off balance at all times, that way they would never be able to hurt us. I'm just not sure that leadership style works with my generation or the generation that is emerging as teenagers today. My generation has seen enough of the plastic, guarded, and inauthentic leader. We're looking for someone who is not afraid to *not* know everything, but *is* willing to teach you what they do know.

As I mentioned before, if the young leaders around us can think like we think about ministry situations, they'll make decisions like we would in future ministry situations. Thus, streamlining the decision-making process and eliminating bottlenecks that clog up progress, growth, and expansion.

Mike Ash, our associate pastor, is a great example of a young leader who really found his wings through the leadership freedom he experienced in our up-the-middle reality. As I eluded to earlier in the book, when we moved to southwest Florida, Mike was a talented and gifted twenty-one year old with a pastor's heart bigger than mine. He was rough around the edges, but teachable and adaptable.

Since 2002, Mike has grown exponentially as a leader and now holds tremendous influence with the people of our church and with me. Mike has complete decision-making discretion in our organization on my behalf. He is able to make any decision without needing my approval. Because I let Mike get inside my head in the early days, and let him know how I make decisions in our organization, he now multiplies my leadership ability on a daily basis.

5. *Don't just work—bless them.*

Be as generous as possible to the young leaders around you. The truth is, many in my generation are simply looking for the mom or dad they never had. I was blessed to have great parents who were supportive of me and the dreams I've had. However, many in my generation have not. They are looking to their leaders to play that role in their lives.

There are a number of ways to let the young leaders around you know you care, even when you're small and can't give them money. Give them time. Give them books. Send them places. Have them over to your house. Let them hang out with your kids. Let them tell you their dreams. Young leaders are longing for a leader to listen to their heart and not just be concerned with fulfilling the dream in our heart.

Now that's the truth!

6. *Don't' just work—give them room to fly.*

The best thing you can do is show young leaders that you trust them. Begin releasing ministry opportunities to your young leaders. Nothing will communicate your trust and belief in them like responsibility. One of the greatest moments for me as a leader is when a young leader on our team takes a chance and succeeds!

Elizabeth, one of our worship leaders in the making, is a seventeen year old fireball who has the ability to turn the world upside down. Last Easter, during worship, she stepped forward and challenged our people to encounter God like they never had before! God showed up in an unprecedented way because of her faith in that moment! I stood there on the front row with tears in my eyes, blown away by the fact that God would trust us with such an amazing young talent! As a leader, there's truly no better feeling.

7. Don't just work them–release them.

One of the great pieces of advice I received early in ministry is to *hold no one tightly.* From our beginning, we have adopted that mindset when it comes to developing leaders around us. In our previous ministry experiences, we never saw leaders have a willingness to release young leaders into new and greater things. Therefore, we have always wanted to model what we felt like we never had. Is it difficult? Sure, but it has resulted in amazing blessings as we have *held no one tightly.*

Our faith has been built up in those moments where we didn't know what we would do without them. In those moments, God always has a way of providing and raising up just the right person or persons to fill the hole we may have felt in our church. Allow God to stretch you and your leadership by developing the leaders around you with the mindset that they will not be with you forever. Impart into them that which will bless the leader they will work with next. If you'll do that, God will always keep your leadership pipeline full.

Concluding Thoughts on Growing Future Superstars

In closing out this section on the people of the up-the-middle church, let me just remind you that it takes time. Don't rush the process with your young leaders—enjoy it. I have often wondered if we could have been bigger, faster, if we would have had more seasoned leaders. What I've discovered is that having the privilege of putting our DNA into the young leaders at NLC positions us to multiply our effectiveness in the future and goes way beyond just having a bigger church in the present. By investing in young leaders, we're impacting the future exponentially!

Up-the-middle churches have the ability to provide the training, opportunity, and platform for young leaders to grow and develop like few other church environments can today. You have been given a unique opportunity to surround yourself with some of the freshest, brightest, and most passionate voices in the body of Christ today! Believe in them, trust them, and pour into them everything you know about church and ministry life. Then sit back and learn from them as well!

Chapter 10

Questions for the Huddle

Discussion Starters for Teams

1. Is your church creating an environment that is attracting young leaders? Spend some time as a team discussing how you strategically create space for young leaders in the future.

2. Do young leaders have access to how the key leaders in your church think about leadership and decision-making? Spend some time as a team strategizing how to create those opportunities.

3. Are you celebrating when a young leader takes a risk, regardless of whether they succeed or fail? Spend some time as a team talking about how you can create a culture of risk and celebration.

Section 4

The Personal Side of the Up-the-Middle Church

"Effective spiritual ministry flows out of being, and God is concerned with our being. He is forming it."

- The Making of a Leader - J. Robert Clinton

I believe that longevity in ministry is largely determined by mastering the art of self-care. In an up-the-middle reality, the stakes are high, and having a grasp on one's personal life will make or break you.

Chapter 11

Staying & Playing Healthy

Up-the-middle pastors stay on top of their game

How many times have we seen it happen—today's great church leader is tomorrow's victim to moral failure. Why is it we can attend entire conferences on how to grow our churches, have greater influence, and make a greater impact for God in our cities, and yet hear nothing on this issue that is literally eroding the credibility of the American church? The truth is that the success of any ministry can be toppled by one leader having something small and seemingly *insignificant* out of balance in his personal life.

It's not enough for self-care in a leader's life to be an after thought or luxury. We, the leaders in the church world, have it especially difficult. In a smaller church reality, we're the primary drivers of the entire organization. We feel the burden of added pressures, stressors, and attacks from the enemy attempting to kill this thing while it is still small.

I've learned a lot about self-care since launching Next Level Church in 2002. Much of my desire for learning on this idea of self-care came as a response to so much of what I had seen in ministry prior to moving to Southwest Florida. A lot of extremes and imbalances in leaders' lives that eventually became lids to their ministry potential. Seeing the extremes propelled me to attempt to do ministry differently than

I had seen it modeled before. What follows are several thoughts on the issue of self-care. May they motivate each of us to keep our lives and ministries functioning out of the overflow of God's Spirit in our hearts.

1. *Be okay with getting away.*

My staff will tell you I'm notorious for saying that *"Church happens every seven days whether we like it or not."* Ministry is so weekly. You've already heard me call it the "Monster of Sunday." Whether we like it or not, Sunday's coming, and Sunday can have a way of nipping at our heals if we don't stay on top of it.

One of the pressures I know many face is the feeling that they can't be gone. I have known pastors who have become so overwhelmed by this pressure that they literally have not taken a Sunday off in years. If they take a family vacation, they'll either schedule it from Monday to Saturday, or even worse, fly back on Saturday and leave their family on vacation without them.

One of the biggest keys to self-care is being okay with getting away. From the beginning of our church, we wanted to set two priorities in motion that we believed would make a big difference concerning the culture of Next Level Church. The first was to set the precedent that I'm not the only one who can speak into the lives of our people. We knew it was important for our church people to be okay with someone, other than myself, speaking into their lives.

The second priority was to show them it was okay for their pastor to be gone. We wanted our people to understand that the church wouldn't completely fall apart, because I missed a Sunday. In fact, we have a couple in our church who have been with us since our first Sunday, and every time I'm with them, they joke that they have attended our church more than I have. As a leader of an up-the-middle church, you have the ability to create a precedent of it being okay for you to be away every once in a while. Don't miss the opportunity to teach your people and empower your leadership base to step up and carry the ball while their pastor takes time to rest and be away.

I'm beginning to define my rhythm for speaking at Next Level. What I've come to realize is that I am good for about six Sundays, and then I need a Sunday off. Whether that's speaking in another church, or just being at Next Level but letting someone else speak, I've found that my rhythm for speaking is about six weeks on and one week off. Maybe you're not at a place to do this right now, but let me encourage you to start somewhere.

Another thought on taking time off is to not be afraid to get away for conferences during the year. I recommend building this into the church's budget from day one. Putting yourself in a position to see other ministries who are further ahead than you will keep your ministry fresh for the long-term. Going a day early or staying a day later can often give you the ability to stay over in that city and visit a church or two. Take advantage of those opportunities.

I know for me, there's nothing like a road trip to bring about fresh ideas of inspiration. Some of the greatest stories I've ever told have come from an experience I've had while traveling outside my city limits. You'll be amazed at what you think about while you're thinking about nothing.

Getting away can also be considered a study break, which was popularized by Bill Hybels, I believe. Presently, thousands of pastors all over the world are reaping the benefits from it. As I've said before in this book, ministry isn't like any other business on the planet. What we do every week requires that we be fresh, creative, and anointed. Those three qualities don't happen by sitting in an office for fifty-two weeks a year. They happen by strategically building into our yearly calendar some time to get out of the daily grind, and into the heart of God.

If you are early on into your ministry, don't miss the opportunity to build in a study break. Even if it's just a day or two in the beginning, get the precedence set. If your board won't go for it, then you either haven't explained it well enough, or you have the wrong people on the board. Creativity flows from extended periods of uninterrupted thought. A study break is a great place to get a few of those. (I have written eight messages in three days over a study break before.)

If you're a ways into your up-the-middle journey, then I highly recommend you begin to carve in a study break as soon as possible. Truth is, it's already long over due. Connect with the powers that be to get it cleared. The long-term creativity of your church depends on it. Church happens every seven days, and that pace can be grueling even for the best leaders. So begin now and get away. The long-term payoff is worth it.

2. *Find a hobby.*

Being in the people-building business is what we're doing isn't it? I mean, really, we just flat out love this stuff, don't we? We eat it, breathe it, sleep it, wake up in the middle of the night thinking about it, and love it! The danger, however, lies in it becoming all we think about and do. And whether we realize it or not, that can turn into a bad thing over time. Far too many leaders drift into ill-health because of a lack of a hobby.

I have to have a diversion. Something in my life that is completely separate from ministry and church work. Something I can get caught up in that is not illegal, unethical, or immoral.

For me it's baseball. One great thing about baseball is that for six months a year, it happens everyday. Something changes every single day. That means I have the ability to divert from my world for a little while and see what's happening outside of Next Level Church. I have even set a goal to see a major league game in all thirty stadiums in the major leagues. (I'm always looking or new friends in *Major League* cities.)

What you do for a hobby doesn't matter. What does matter is that you find a hobby. Something you can get lost in for a little while every so often. Include your wife in on this if you can. Even if she has no interest in what it is, you can at least let her know why it's so important for you to be into it. For my 30th birthday, our church sent my wife and I to San Francisco to knock out two more stadiums… how fun and we missed a Sunday! Creating a diversion from ministry is a huge part of self-care.

3. *Have a life outside of church.*

He Builds it!
P= 14

In ministry, church is life. Outside of ministry, church is something you do on Sunday for an hour or two. Early on, we got a piece of advice from a prominent Christian leader who told us, *"Don't take yourself too seriously, no one else does."* I love that. It is essential to keep ministry in perspective. After all, Jesus said that *He* would build his church and the gates of hell would not prevail against it. Yet it's so tempting to start thinking that it's us. Release the wheel. Keep giving Jesus the control. That means having a life outside of *what you do*.

Resist the guilt that comes from not carrying the burden 24/7. Even after all these years of leading a church, I still struggle with this. In fact, I felt that way just this morning. I went out for a prayer walk at 6 am. It was the first day back after a holiday weekend, and the first thought I had when I hit the street was, *"God, I know I haven't really been working on the church over the past few days."* (I actually took a few days off over the weekend and spent the time with my wife and kids.)

So there I was on my prayer walk feeling guilty. It took me several minutes to work through it and focus on what really mattered.

Taking command over the feeling that you have to constantly be *doing it* or *carrying it* is one of the most difficult things we must learn to do. It's also one of the healthiest things we'll do. After all, no one has to convince us that this is the most important "business" on the planet. So for us to stop working on it for a day or two can be border-line overwhelming.

Early in my ministry, I actually had a leader tell me, "Satan doesn't take a day off… so why should we?" We have to know that Satan capitalizes on this. He will kick our tail with feelings of guilt over not being 100% *in* it all the time. He'll tell us things like, *"No wonder your church isn't growing like you want it to. You aren't taking it seriously enough or working hard enough on it."* He'll put thoughts in our head like, *"Jesus died for this, and you can't give up a Saturday or two?"* or *"God never sleeps but you want a day off each week?"* When we give in to these thoughts and start believing them, they eventually lead us to burnout, which is right where Satan wants us to be. Burned out. Used up. Of no good to anyone… church, people, family, wife, kids, anyone. And yet, so many of us can't move past the guilt in order to actually lay the burden down long enough to get some rest and care for ourselves. If we want to lead long-term in an up-the-middle reality, we must have a life outside of church. Don't let the voice of past leaders or even worse, Satan keep you from having a full life.

4. Take a Day Off.

In my ministry training, I was taught to never let the business world out work us. What that meant was, don't worry about burning the candle at both ends; just keep the fire going, even if you have to burn every last ounce of everything you've got. Don't stop working

136

in ministry. In fact, we were actually told that Sunday wasn't a *work* day; it was a *ministry* day, and since everyone else was volunteering, so should we. It was our *service* to God. Man, I'm glad God has helped me break free from so much of that thinking into a more life-giving model of ministry. If you have been taught something similar to that, let me give you permission to forsake that advice. It will kill you, your family, and your ministry, which I suppose is exactly what Satan is hoping for.

About five months into the church's existence, my wife and I began to look at my schedule and realize that this pastoring thing had the potential to overtake my schedule with meetings, planning, studying, and networking in the community. We forced ourselves to take a good hard look at our family and marriage priorities. The result was to draw some hard boundary lines while the church was still small. Looking back, it's the best move we ever made.

The first thing we did was determine that Friday would be my day off. I'll be honest with you; this was tough for me. It took me about ten or twelve weeks to actually get my schedule adjusted to where I had no appointments on Fridays and where I could mentally wind down my week by Thursday afternoon. But once we settled into that rhythm, we have never looked back. It has been the best decision we ever made.

Do whatever it takes to keep yourself from working on your day off. Rob Bell describes his day off as "A day without lists." I love that. I covet my Fridays. They have truly become a day of rest for me. And what I have found is that by Saturday, I'm actually relaxed. If I can keep my Saturdays relatively clear, then I actually feel like I have a weekend like the rest of the world. Two days off in a row. It's a great feeling. It helps me to come into Sunday rested and ready to go.

Some of my pastor friends take Mondays off. I think that's great for them, but for me, I know my week won't get done if it doesn't start on Monday. I've also found that if I can get in and get a great start on my week on Monday, then the rest of my week goes much more smoothly. I'm a better leader, boss, pastor, husband, and dad when I feel under control on Monday, rather than when I feel the monster of Sunday nipping at my heals. Regardless of the day you choose, do yourself, your family, and your church a favor and take a day off. (And don't be afraid to take a nap.)

5. *Work hard on Your Marriage.*

I believe there to be no greater strain on a marriage than the ministry. Unfortunately, ministry has killed more marriages than any of us would like to admit. If we don't fight like crazy to protect our marriages, ministry has the potential to destroy them. If we don't fight for our marriages, no one else will! It's up to us not to let the ministry become the mistress.

Since we started Next Level Church in 2002, my wife and I have experienced something that I believe few couples ever get to experience together. We have seen God take our marriage to a level of intimacy and passion that, quite frankly, I didn't even know existed. About a year and half into our planting the church, I had a friend of mine from Ohio come down for a few days just to hang out, swap stories, and golf. During our time together, he got in my face about settling for the status quo in my marriage. The thing was that mine and Sarah's relationship was in fine shape at the time. But he was persistent...

When I say he got in my face, I'm not exaggerating. He literally sat my wife and I down (talk about awkward) and said, "I know you guys think that what you have right now is, 'good,' but I'm telling you, it can be way better. Don't settle in your marriage. Go deeper." He literally

138

put our friendship on the line in order to push us to greater places in our marriage. (He later told me that when he got on the plane to leave the next morning, he wasn't sure if he would ever see me again. But five years later, he joined our staff!)

Over the next few weeks, Sarah and I found ourselves with a new-found permission to question, wonder, and desire something greater in our marriage. Where we have ended up has been nothing short of spectacular! So, regardless of the present state of your marriage, I want to give you permission to look deeper right now!

Too many times we put *Christian Marriage* in a box. We pigeon-hole our marriages into these conservative, lifeless places that lack fun, creativity, and don't honor God. What if God wants to smile and sing over your marriage like the Bible describes? What if God desires for you and your spouse to keep on pursuing one another like He keeps on pursuing His bride? Listen, if you need someone to give you permission to start believing that there could be more in marriage, then: consider this permission granted! You have total access to believe God to take your marriage to places you've never been before. If you need help, get it. Seek out a marriage counselor. As you'll hear in my story later, there's no shame in admitting that you weren't born with all the answers. God gives certain people knowledge and gifts to be able to help other people (like us) figure out how God made us to think and be. Just because we're pastors doesn't mean we have to believe the lie that we are supposed to know everything and have all the answers.

If you and your wife need to have some conversations, have them. Let it get awkward. Let it get uncomfortable. Because on the other side of that uncomfortable place is an unbelievable place that God has designed for the two of you. (If you have a knot in your stomach right now, then this section is for you. Have your spouse read this. Then have a talk.)

Have together time or...date-night.

You've heard me use the term *rhythm* several times throughout this book, and at the risk of overusing it, I'm about to use it again. As I mentioned earlier in this chapter, you've got to discover your rhythm in your ministry. Your marriage is no different. If you don't *make* time for one another, it won't happen. The grind of the up-the-middle church will push it right out.

Your marriage is your #1 priority. The reason for this is simple: *If your marriage fails, so will your kids, and so will your ministry.* Too many pastors are guilty of prioritizing the ministry over their marriage. Of course, we all say we don't, but too often the theory is easier to believe than the practice.

As the pastor of an up-the-middle church, you must set a precedent in place in your schedule that time and attention for your spouse is not optional. For my wife and I, we have discovered that our rhythm for face-to-face extended together time is about two weeks. Therefore, we plan on going out about every other Friday night. There are a few exceptions that come up every once in a while, but for the most part, every two weeks, we get a few hours of alone time that we have come to determine is priceless.

Let me encourage you to find your rhythm for your together time. This may require some time to perfect, but it is well worth it. When your spouse begins to realize they are as high of a priority as everyone else who gets a slot on your calendar, it will do wonders for the trust factor in your marriage.

There will always be a dozen excuses why you can't have a date-night. No Money. No Babysitters. No Time. Excuses are out there. Don't let them stop you. In fact, if your spouse sees you working hard to make date-night happen, it will add great value to your marriage.

I remember when we first began to really prioritize our date-night. I had to be the one to find the babysitter. I'm not sure if my wife was testing me to see if it was really a priority or what, but for whatever reason, she would let the babysitter detail slide. So, after a couple of weeks of this, I just took matters into my own hands and decided to figure it out. I figured that my wife needed to see me breaking my back for her as much as I did for a family in the church that was *in need.* And it worked! Her face would light up when I said, "I've got it all taken care of..."

Limit your nights out of the house

Another aspect of defining a rhythm in your marriage has to do with the number of nights out per week. In leading an up-the-middle church, there will be a definite temptation to be *out* every night of the week.

This was the other half of the conversation my wife and I had concerning my schedule in the early stages of our church plant. We began to realize that if we weren't proactive about setting limitations to my evening activities with the church or people, I could literally be gone every night of the week. So that's what we did. We looked at our weekly schedule and decided that, as a rule, I would limit my nights away from home each week to no more than three. Of course, there would be exceptions to that, but for the most part, that would be our standard.

We also determined we would do our best to make sure that three out of the other four nights would include dinner around the table together as a family. This was a priority in my family growing up. My mom had dinner on the table at 5:30 every night, whether we were there or not. That example served us well as we began to define family parameters during the early days of our church. Some of the best communication with our kids happens around our dinner table. It is important to keep that precedent set in our home.

I was having lunch a few months ago with a friend who pastors a church about the same size as ours and this topic came up. I began to share with him about the conversation my wife and I had had nearly three years ago. Over the next few minutes, he shared that he and his wife were struggling to find one night per week when the entire family was home together. So if you need to make a change, don't wait. If we're not careful to establish those parameters, our weekly schedule can lead us to ill-health.

Define the purpose of "getting together" with people

[handwritten margin note: Ang is more of this]

Another great conversation my wife and I had about two years into the church was about meetings with people. I'm a people person, so meeting and connecting with people is something that energizes me and gets me excited. In the early days of our church, meeting with people was a great way to share the vision of the church and get to know them. My wife and I were privileged to connect with so many people in our church at that time.

However, after the birth of our second son, my wife began to pull back from some of this *connecting* that I was so excited about. I remember having a great conversation with her after a new couple had contacted me, desiring to have lunch with us. Sarah shared with me how she couldn't keep attending all of my meetings *and* get everything done. She also communicated that it wasn't fair to drag our boys out every time someone wanted to meet with their dad and mom.

Sarah encouraged me to begin doing the preliminary homework of finding out why people wanted to meet with us. If they just desired to get to know me and my wife and hear our heart for the church, then they probably needed to start by meeting with me over coffee, not spending an evening with both of us. We weren't in a position to be friends with everyone in our church anymore. We needed to be *pastors*, not necessarily *friends* with everyone.

Being friends with every new couple just wasn't going to work. We couldn't be true to the friendships and relationships that were key to us (like with staff members and their spouses, or key leaders in the church) and be friends with everyone else, as well. We had to begin prioritizing our friendships and trust that people would pursue relationships through our connection groups.

The other side of the issue for me, as a man, was that I loved having my wife next to me in a meeting. She has a personality that people immediately fall in love with. So, for me, this took some adjusting to. I had to become more confident in my ability to connect with people. I personally had to adjust to the reality that I was not called to be everyone's friend, and that people don't need me to be their friend, as much as they need me to be their pastor. I'm the kind of guy that meets someone at Starbucks, and is planning a family vacation with them by the end of the conversation. However, I can't tell you how liberating it was for me and our family when I finally embraced this differentiation. It was better for our church people, our friends, and our family.

Keep growing in your marriage

One of the amazing things that happened after my buddy from Ohio gave us our "Come to Jesus marriage meeting," was that we had permission to keep pursuing knowledge about marriage and male and female "stuff" in general. This quest for greater knowledge has yielded amazing benefits in our understanding of each other.

There are two must-read books for any couple who wants to grow in their marriage. The information included in these two small books is enough content to keep you busy for a year of date-nights. Take one chapter at a time, read it individually, and then talk about it on your date. It will blow your mind. *For Women Only* and *For Men Only* by Shaunti and Jeff Feldhahn have the power to change your marriage forever. My wife found Shaunti's book after that conversation with our friend from Ohio. It brought clarity to so much of hwat we were feeling and has changed our marriage for the better. When it comes to doing ministry up-the-middle, it is essential to keep your marriage a priority and keep growing.

6. Get and Keep Your Finances in Order

The ministry is a tough place to wrestle with the area of personal finances. Getting your personal financial house in order will position you to be exponentially more effective in facing an up-the-middle reality. Too many pastors have never taken the time to educate themselves on how to handle their finances effectively and consequently have fallen prey to the world's agenda. Here are a few tips on managing your personal finances:

1. **Keep your debt load low.** The #1 piece of advice I give to church planters and pastors who find themselves in an up-the-middle church reality is to get and stay out of debt. The American dream tells us to arrange our life in such a way that it gives off the appearance of affluence. As a pastor in an up-the middle-reality, you won't have the luxury of carrying a huge amount of debt with you. If you've got to have a salary that allows you to pay a bunch of monthly payments on credit cards and car payments each month, it's going to be really difficult to be effective.

   God has blessed my wife and I in that we have never (ever) carried credit card debt. We use credit cards to get the free stuff you can redeem with points (like free coffee at Starbucks) but we have always paid off our credit cards in full at the end of every month. If you can't pay it off at the end of the month, you can't afford to purchase whatever it is that you're buying.

A quick side note for those who may be thinking of starting a church: If you have a lot of debt, you may want to put off the start of your church until you can eliminate the vast majority of that debt. Church planting is hard enough without the added stress of personal financial indebtedness. If you have credit card debt, begin now to get rid of all your consumer debt, and begin disciplining yourself to never pay interest on a credit card again. It's plain and simple, you will never get where God wants you to go paying interest on credit cards.

The truth is that the way a person handles their personal finances will be the way they handle the church's finances, as well. That's another reason why this is such a huge deal for up-the-middle churches. It can't be understated; being a good steward in the area of personal finances is a really big deal.

2. **Keep your monthly expenses low.** If there is one thing that God has allowed me and Sarah to do, it's to keep our monthly bills low. We knew that to be free to plant a church, we needed to have minimal monthly bills. We knew supporting two car payments, full insurance, and gas and maintenance each month would make it tough to church plant effectively. If you have school debt that requires a monthly payment, get it paid off. Carrying the weight of debt only adds the weight of doing church up-the-middle.

3. **Build in Margin.** One way to get and stay ahead financially in ministry, even when you don't make a lot of money, is to learn to build in margin in your personal finances. If you can give a tithe and save a tithe and live on 80%, you'll be doing great. Dave Ramsey says it this way, *"If you will live like no one else, later you can live like no one else."* For a pastor, living "like no one else" isn't

about a grand lifestyle as much as it is about living the dream of ministry! Margin is huge. Do without if you have to. Do whatever it takes to live on 80% or less of your income.

4. **Be a generous giver.** Hopefully you've discovered the joy of generous giving in your life by now. If not, begin now. Start praying for God to put a spirit of generosity in your heart. Begin reading about it, and then begin writing checks! Sarah and I have always lived generously. We have always tried to give, not only 10% to the church, but above and beyond as God leads us. We count it a privilege to be used by God to channel money into Kingdom causes. There is no better feeling we have all month, than when we get to bless someone and give money away to help others! Live generously. God will bless you for it. In an up-the-middle reality, you need all the blessing you can get!

5. **Be willing to sacrifice.** Ministry has never been a get rich scheme. If you're pastoring because of the money, find something else to do. You'll work way too hard and be compensated far too little to do this for any length of time. The people business is a rewarding one…just not necessarily in a monetary way!

After several years in an up-the-middle reality, my wife and I still aren't up to the same pay scale as some other pastors who took over existing churches, and that's perfectly okay with us. In fact, at multiple moments in our church history, we have willingly given up a pay raise in order to add another staff member. We feel that by paying others to focus on the church with us, we can multiply our efforts. The day will come when we're compensated accurately for what we do. But we leave that in God's hands. He's hasn't failed us yet.

Concluding Thoughts on Self-Care

Self-care for pastors looks like getting a handle on all that we have talked through in this chapter. These elements are a great launch pad for personal health and wholeness as you do church up-the-middle.

If you don't take care of yourself, no one else will. As the new normal in the church world, doing church up-the-middle is a dog-eat-dog world, and as we're all too aware of the pressures and demands that can be overwhelming. Having personal priorities for yourself will position you for long-term success in your life and ministry.

Chapter 11

Questions for the Huddle

Discussion Starters for Teams

1. Are you placing adequate priority on the health of your lead pastor and other key leaders? Spend some time as a team discussing how you can protect the health of the lead pastor and his family.

2. How are the marriages of the leaders of your church? Spend some time as a team getting honest about the strength and health of the marriages of your leaders.

3. What adjustments need to be made to the program and calendar of the church in order to allow for the leadership to play and stay healthy long-term. Spend some time as a team cutting, eliminating and tweaking programming to make it more manageable long-term.

Chapter 12

Playing inside the Lines

Up-the-middle pastors define clear and healthy boundaries in their personal lives

So much of what we've learned by leading an up-the-middle church has to do with the personal life of the pastor. It really is true that the success or failure of a church will be in direct proportion to the ability of the lead pastor (and his team) to manage his personal life effectively. If the wheels fall off at home, the wheels fall off of the church. Let me say it another way...

I began this section by stating that I believe longevity in ministry is largely dependent on learning the art of self-care. Ministry is tough, and ministry in an up-the-middle reality is even more difficult. It's exhausting. It's wearying. It's demanding and it's thankless. It really is true that only the strong survive. If we aren't aggressive in our pursuit of personal health and wholeness, no one else will be. The essence of the people business is TAKE. The writer of proverbs was almost completely right when he said, *"There are three things that are never satisfied, four that never say, 'Enough!': the grave, the barren womb, land, which is never satisfied with water, and fire, which never says, 'Enough!'"*

Personally, I'm tempted to add *Church People* to his list! Of course, not all church people, but some people. You know...the ones who WANT their pastor's time, energy, and attention 24/7! For them, it's all about the WANT, isn't it? The truth is, people can *want* us to death in ministry, and yet, of all the people that we need to care for in a week's time, none are more important than ourselves. The most important person to take care of in ministry is you.

So what does that look like in an up-the-middle reality? When we're in a reality where so much is on the line, how do we set boundaries to protect the health of ourselves and our families? How do we set valuable precedents in place that will stay with us throughout the life of our ministry and our church? Here are a few of my most current thoughts on boundaries that must be set to succeed in an up-the-middle church.

1. *Learn the Art of Saying No.*

Saying no can be one of the most difficult things for an up-the-middle church leader to do. There are many reasons for this. First, if your church is young or small, you know your presence at events is huge. You *are* the face of the church in many ways. There's a good chance you feel all kinds of pressure, some real and some imagined, to be present. And yet, if you don't begin drawing boundaries now that communicate that it is okay for the pastor, his wife, and their family to *not* be at everything, it will set you, your family, and your church up for tremendous difficulty later.

When our church was two years old and had about 200 people, I remember a couple pulling me and my wife aside and telling us how upset they were that we had failed to attend a small group meeting they were at the previous weekend. When I explained to them that it would be impossible for me and my wife to be at all of our small groups' special events, they replied, "Well, we just don't know if we can attend a church where the pastor and his family aren't at every event." They left the church a short time later.

I understand drawing this boundary is easier said than done. I have been on the receiving end of those conversations, and it's tough to swallow. All I can say is, let them leave. If they're really that fickle, then you can't build a strong, lasting ministry on people like that anyway. I know God will bring you people who will honor your family time and not put that pressure on you.

Ed Young, Jr. has given some great advice: *"Pastor your church as if it's twice the size."* We began doing this when our church was fifty people, and it has served us well. It helped us put boundaries in place with our time and presence that we continue to reap benefits from. Don't do at 100 what you can't do at 200.

Let's look at a principle from the other side of the coin: It's possible to *fly over* your current reality and severely damage your church. I have coached many pastors who are not pastoring in reality. They think that because the vision is huge in their head and heart, then they need to act that way now. Consequently, they preach like there are 5,000 people in the room when there are actually eighty. Every element of a church must transition as the church grows. Worship for 5,000, or even 500, doesn't work with seventy or eighty people. Preaching style, availability, and structures of ministry all must transition as the church grows.

One of the greatest mistakes you can make in leading an up-the-middle church is to pretend you're something you're not. When I talk about pastoring your church as if it's twice it's size, it doesn't mean we can allow ourselves to get haughty about it. It can become easy to start thinking that you're more than you really are. As a church of 100 people, the pastor must be more present than when the church is 500.

Don't let yourself run to the extreme of, *"Well, someday we're going to have 5,000 people on six campuses, so we better not have dinner with that new couple because we won't be able to then."* Give yourself permission to be where you are in your church-growth journey. Be all there mentally; otherwise, you'll end up selling your people short in the process. (And you'll sell yourself short in learning all that God has for you at your present level.)

2. *Don't answer your cell phone all the time.*

Cell phones can be huge blessings at times, but they can also become a hindrance in your process of self-care. It happened to me one time, and I don't want it to happen again. We were sitting at dinner, and my phone rang. My oldest son looked at my pocket where my phone was and said, "not again." In that moment, I knew I had to draw a boundary with my phone. If we're not careful, our wife and kids will come to resent our cell phone.

Let me explain a little further. As I've stated in earlier chapters, we are in the people-building business. That means there is *always* something going on. Why? Because in the people business, people have problems, and, as if that's not enough, Sunday happens every seven days, whether we like it or not. Because of that, the details are always coming. AND... people have jobs during the day, so the only time they can really talk is at night. However, if we can't reign in our cell phone, it will eventually take over our life.

When we started the church, my cell phone *was* the church phone. It was on our website, printed in our bulletin, and even in the phone book that way! (There are still a couple of websites that have it listed. We can't seem to get it changed. So on Sunday mornings, when my cell phone rings, I've learned to answer it, "Next Level Church, may I help you?" Most of the time, it's someone wanting to know when our service times are. It's hilarious!)

Let me state this as plainly as I know how: *I own my cell phone; my cell phone does not own me.* Those are words for every pastor to live by.

While we're at it, here's another one: *One man's emergency is another man's inconvenience.* Probably one of the most important conversations you can have with your spouse is about your cell phone.

If there is one thing I want my wife and kids to know, it's that they are more important than my cell phone. In other words, when I'm with them, nothing is more important than they are in that moment. I'll even tell them that. If they hear my phone ring, and I don't answer it, they'll sometimes ask me why not. These are great moments to reinforce in your kids that, "In this moment, you're #1." It doesn't mean that you don't listen to the messages and call people back, but it does look like a boundary stake you nail down as soon as possible. I'll even tell people why I didn't pick up earlier. "I'm sorry I couldn't get to your call, I was having dinner with my kids." Let people know they aren't as important in those moments as your family. They'll thank you for the example you set for them.

My wife and kids have open access to me any place, any time, anywhere, and they know it. If I'm in a lunch appointment and my wife calls through, no matter what, I get it. (The flip side is, she knows this, and is respectful of where I am and doesn't take advantage of it.) If I'm in a meeting in my office with someone, and she needs me for something, she knows that she is always allowed to knock and enter without question. (Again, she is great about not taking advantage of this. She wants to be respectful to the people I'm meeting with, as well.) She also has learned over the past fifteen years of doing life and ministry together that I need my quiet and alone time. She understands that in order for me to be creative, I need interruptions to be at a minimum, so when I'm studying, she'll do everything within her power to leave me alone. (She's great like that!)

What about Staff and Other Key People?

Concerning staff and other key leaders that I deem appropriate, I would call my availability to them Level 2. They know they have priority access to me when they need it and can call me at anytime. Of course, I have caller ID, so I can see when it's them. They understand that I will answer as much as possible because they know they are priority for me. However, they also understand that family comes first, and they try to be respectful of that. Also, if I don't answer, and it's truly an emergency (and they know when that is and isn't) then they know to keep calling me. I will usually answer it after the third time. This rarely happens, but it's a great rule for us!

On my day off, I will seldom answer the phone. In the early days, I would actually change my message to say, "Today is my day off. If this is a church-related matter, please leave a message, and I'll get to it when I can. If this is personal, then call my wife's cell phone." But I wouldn't leave the number. That way, anyone who had her number could call it; but anyone else who didn't already have her number couldn't get to us. I'm not trying to be a jerk; I just don't want my cell phone to run my life and invade my family time. Family time in a ministry home is precious and thus, worthy of protection.

You and your family will have to determine a comfortable and acceptable level of availability for you. You're a husband and father first, then a pastor. One friend of mine told me once, "Pastoring this church is what you do in your free time...when you're not being a husband and a father at home!" I love that! Be sure to keep your family #1, not #2. That's easier said than done, especially in an up-the-middle reality.

3. Master the Art of E-mail and Voice-mail.

Both e-mail and voice mail can also run your life if you let them. My advice is, DON'T LET THEM! For me, creativity flows from uninterrupted blocks of time when I can meet with Jesus, pray, write, and think. If I am constantly being interrupted by phone calls and e-mails, those great thoughts of inspiration quickly fade back to the to-do list. Determine three times in your day when you will check and return e-mails and phone calls, and then stick to that. This will give you the freedom to know that those urgent things will get dealt with. It will just happen on your time, not someone else's. Just remember that it would probably do a world of good to figure out how to turn the "bing-bong" off that let's you know every time you get a new e-mail. For someone with ADD, that's just a disaster waiting to happen. I had to figure out how to nip that in the bud quickly. I can't have all those stimulations happening all at once, or I'll never be able to concentrate long enough to actually hear from God.

Learn the art of leaving messages, too. Communicate to those close to you the importance of leaving you a detailed message. A lot of ground can be covered that way. Teach them to not just say, "This is Matt. Call me when you get a chance." Let people know that the more information they can leave, the better. A tremendous amount of work can be done toward a solution to the problem before you ever call someone back. If you're really close to someone, you can deal with an entire situation without ever talking at all. Just leaving messages back and forth can be a great way to get things done, on your timetable, not someone else's. Texting applies as well. However, again, the little alert noise can become absolutely addictive, if you're not careful. Shut if off. (Say it out loud... Shut. It. Off.) The world will not stop spinning if you don't get a text for an hour or two. Being available through e-mail and text is great, but it can block creativity if you let it.

Concluding Thoughts on Boundaries

If you're in the beginning phases of a new church, then you have a unique season of opportunity to set precedents now that will stay with you and your church for years to come. Even if you're in an existing up-the-middle church reality, making some changes to the boundaries of your personal life will position you to go up-the-middle more effectively in the future. Start with having some big conversations with your spouse, staff, and family members. Then together, begin making the big decisions that will protect your health, the health of your family, and the health of your church for the long-run.

Chapter 12

Questions for the Huddle

Discussion Starters for Teams

1. What underlying beliefs do you have about the *availability* of the key leaders of a church? Spend some time as a team talking about the boundaries that are or are not in place to protect the health of key leaders.

2. How well do you say no? Spend some time as a team getting honest about the temptation to be available to everybody all of the time.

3. What are the areas of your life right now that are draining you and making you less effective as a leader? Spend some time as a team discussing how you can help one another manage these areas and increase productivity.

Chapter 13

Being Head Coach

My up-the-middle story of getting real and living whole

"Why do you look at the speck of sawdust in someone else's eye
and pay no attention to the plank in your own eye?"

- Jesus

Pastors are supposed to have all the answers, right? I mean, people come to us with problems, and we help them fix those problems. That's what we do. We help people, right? The danger in that line of thinking is that we can become blind to the condition of our own hearts. I believe Jesus once said something about a speck and a plank. Apparently, I can't remember too well since I've only been seeing out of one eye for quite sometime...

I'm not okay.

In the year 2000, while we were still living up north, I had a life-changing experience—a moment that has changed the direction of my life, my marriage, and my ministry in a profound way. Let me explain. My wife and I were on a date. We had enjoyed a nice dinner and then found ourselves at the movie theater watching a movie about a couple who was struggling in their marriage. While I sat there watching the movie, the Holy Spirit was convicting my heart about my own life and marriage.

Sarah and I had been married about three and a half years at the time, and things were great. No kids, but our plans were heading in that direction. We were traveling and doing national youth ministry. We had a house, a cat, and even had a great car, but I sat in that movie theater next to my wife knowing that something in my heart wasn't right. Something was out of balance. I was not okay. I had allowed some unhealthy thought patterns and behaviors to creep into my life. It was time to come clean.

When the movie was over, we went to a nearby restaurant for dessert. I can remember feeling sick to my stomach as I was sitting there. I finally just blurted it out to my wife. "I'm not okay. God has been convicting me all night that if I don't deal with this stuff in my heart, it will eventually destroy our marriage, our ministry, and our potential." I honestly can't remember how the remainder of the conversation went. I know my wife was an absolute champ. I think I remember her trying to encourage me and love me and say something hope-filled. The truth is, I was one hurting man. Even at the age of 24, ministry had taken its toll on me, and I wasn't okay.

It's okay to not be okay

Coming off our conversation, my wife and I agreed that I should begin seeing a counselor. Through the recommendation of a friend, I connected with a guy who was a Christian mental health counselor. His name was John. I wasn't quite sure of what I was doing, or what I would say, but I knew that the stuff I was dealing with in my heart was producing unhealthy patterns of behavior in my life, and I needed someone to help me sort it all out.

I can remember the first few times I went to talk to this guy; I felt such shame and embarrassment. Where I came from in ministry, pastors don't get help. Counselors are for the weak; pastors fix themselves. We don't admit we don't know it all. We keep quiet and we certainly don't ask for help. We give it. I remember thinking, "If anyone in my ministry circle finds out I'm seeing a counselor, this could be devastating." But I knew I wasn't okay, and I needed someone outside of my world to help me start going through the junk I had allowed to build up on my heart.

Over a period of several months, John began to help me unpack a lot of the baggage that had been building up in my life for the last couple of decades: stuff from childhood, teen years, and ministry. Basically, things I had seen, experienced, and internalized, instead of processing and letting go. By about the sixth month, I began to realize that even as a pastor, it was okay to not be okay. I was beginning to see the world through a different lens: a lens that was clearer and brighter than anything I had been taught before. I was beginning to move in the direction of personal wholeness, and it felt great. I was beginning to do ministry, marriage, and life from a foundation of wholeness in my heart. This was a new concept for me: a concept I didn't even know was possible.

I went to John every month for two and a half years until we moved to Florida in 2002. I haven't seen or talked to him since. I'd like to. I'd like to tell him what a difference he made in my life, marriage, and ministry. I'd thank him for his courage to *get up in my business* for two and a half years. It was the beginning of my road to wholeness.

I'm not there yet

When we moved to Florida to start the church in 2002, I didn't find a counselor for over a year. But as the pressures of trying to figure out how to plant a church kept piling on, I began to realize I wasn't all the way there yet in my pursuit of wholeness. I hadn't reached a place of wholeness I was satisfied with; therefore, I began to pursue someone else that could take me further.

My search (and God) led me to a guy named Mark. I have to admit that Mark's influence has literally changed my life. He's one of the smartest and toughest question-askers I've ever met. Mark has taught me so much about who I am, who I'm not, and what true success in life is all about. I can truly say that I don't think I would be in ministry today if it weren't for the presence of two men who have worked behind the scenes in my life for nearly a decade now: My counselors John and Mark.

I still see a counselor every month. Having someone in my life who couldn't care less, and couldn't care more has been one of the best investments I've ever made in my life, my marriage, and my ministry. I never knew it could be this good. As pastors, we must understand that it is okay to admit when we're not okay. If that's you, get help. Take action. Your ministry depends on it.

Are you okay?

My hope in sharing my story with you is to give you permission to take an honest look at your life. Too many pastors have spent too long faking out the entire world (including themselves), attempting to convince everyone that they're okay. They've hidden behind big wood desks and big wood pulpits. My heart's desire is that something in my story would inspire you to have the courage to face yourself.

The up-the-middle church reality requires us to face many obstacles: starting whole organizations, moving across the country, taking on demons, and facing the gates of hell, but I contend that for many of us, the biggest obstacle we'll ever face is ourselves. Having the courage to face who we *really* are, where we've *really* come from, and all that we've went through is by far the largest giant we'll ever have to face.

Have you faced yourself?

The only way for your church to become everything God wants for it to be is when you start with the courage to face yourself. If your stomach is in knots right now as you read this, then you're not okay. You're not weak; you're just not okay. And that's okay. It's okay for you to admit you're not okay.

I challenge you to have the courage to tell somebody. Seek out a mental health counselor who knows how God created the human brain and body to work. They can give you insight into why you are the way you are. You'll be a better husband, father, pastor, leader, and friend. I can truly say there is no greater feeling than to pastor and lead people from a foundation of wholeness in my heart. It could be the most important thing you ever do. Perhaps it's time to go up-the-middle into your heart?

A Word about Accountability

Pastoring an up-the-middle church can be one of the loneliest places on the planet. And if we're being honest, accountability can be really hard to come by. The bottom line is this: We need accountability. It is a non-negotiable for an up-the-middle pastor. Our lives are just too difficult, and the pressure is just too great not to have someone in your life that you can be absolutely truthful and honest with.

The reality for each of us is this: We are only as accountable as we want to be. The choice is ours. We can live bound, or we can live free. We can live whole, or we can live a dual reality. I want to challenge you to do whatever it takes to get accountable with someone as soon as possible. There's too much at stake not to.

Chapter 13

Questions for the Huddle

Discussion Starters for Teams

1. What areas of your life are potential landmines that need to be dealt with immediately? Spend some time as a team praying together and challenging one another to live in honest community and seek the help necessary to see every leader living in wholeness.

2. How accountable are you? Spend some time as a team determining how to create levels of accountability for the personal lives of everyone on the team.

3. What will you do to begin moving the people of your church toward honest community as well? Spend some time as a team discussing how to create opportunities for your church people to get real about their personal lives.

Preface to Chapter 14

"The final chapter of this book is by far my favorite. If there is one area where most up-the-middle leaders set themselves up for heartache, it would be this one.

The way we define success will impact every other area of our life and ministry more than anything else we do. This chapter took the longest to write ... probably because it was the hardest for me to learn."

Chapter 14

Winning Your Super Bowl

Up-the-middle churches redefine success in ministry

I don't like to fail. I don't know too many people in ministry who do. Yet one of the hardest things about church work is feeling like you haven't accomplished anything by the end of the day. One of the greatest struggles pastors of up-the-middle churches face is feeling like a failure. I believe the number one reason why new churches fail is unmet expectations: not having experienced what we thought we would. In that moment, the feeling too many of us experience is failure.

Feeling like a failure opens the door to guilt and shame, which then opens the door to embarrassment. We somehow believe we must live up to the expectations of those watching us, and when we don't, we give up. Souls go un-reached. Lives go unchanged. Touchdowns go un-scored. If your journey in ministry hasn't lived up to your expectations and has left you feeling less than successful, then you need a new definition of success.

What is needed most is not to give up, but rather to learn how to redefine success. Perhaps the most valuable lesson we have ever learned has been in the area of how we define success in an up-the-middle reality.

Success Starts with Changing Your Expectations

In the early days of our church plant, we knew it wasn't going to be easy. We didn't have a clue what we were doing. As I remember it, we didn't know what to expect, but because we had been a big fish in our small pond, I think we were hoping it would take off quickly. We thought we would pick up where we left off, so to speak.

Our expectations were that as soon as we got over the initial hump of the launch, it would skyrocket. I remember having a conversation a few months in and saying, "Our three year plan is to be running a thousand people." So yeah, I guess you could say our expectations were pretty high. When we got hooked up with the ARC, we suddenly began to realize there were guys out there who were having the kind of success we thought was possible. However, even after we had implemented the majority of the ARC principles, we still didn't see the exponential growth we had expected.

I remember one day being on my prayer walk and basically crossing a line in my heart. I can remember saying to God, "If this is the journey you have me on, then so be it. I'm okay with not having a long-bomb story. I'm Matt Keller, and I'm okay with that." That was a good day for me. It was the day my expectations changed.

Let me be very clear here when I say that we needed to change our expectations. We have never lowered them, we've just changed them. We still see the huge vision for Next Level Church and all that we believe it can become in the future. However, we have changed our expectations for the here and now. We were finally able to embrace the reality that God is the one who gives the increase. It's His doing, not ours; and it will happen on His timetable, not ours. The minute we can cross that line in our hearts, is the minute we can truly become everything God wants for us (and our church) to become in the present!

KEJ. This has happened to me as well in summer of 2015

167

This hasn't been easy, and it hasn't been a one time deal, either. Since we began in 2002, I've had to 're-cross the line' at multiple points on the journey. It seems like every few months or so, I have to die to my desires for our church to be on my timetable. It almost always comes after a couple of good Sundays in a row! It's usually as I'm driving home from the church that I get this fleeting thought of "This could be it! I think we did it! I think we have finally broken through! This could be our long bomb!" It never fails that the next Sunday attendance is like a record low, and the offerings are brutal. Somehow, that always seems to bring me back down to earth. Expectations changed.

Inaccurate expectations always lead to disappointment and discouragement. This is true of human beings in general. It happens all around us each day. Whenever we fail to experience what we thought we would experience, disappointment is usually the result, and disappointment in an up-the-middle reality can lead to discouragement. Changing our expectations can miraculously heal our discouragement problems.

Success Is Following the "Be All Here!" Concept

I remember one Sunday showing up at the movie theater, unloading some equipment, and then jumping into my car to try and grab a few minutes alone. This was my custom for the first two years. With no place to go inside the movie theater to escape the set up hoopla, I just had to get in my car, drive around to the other side of the mall, and try to focus. I would sit there just long enough to review my notes for my message.

On this particular day, as I drove back around to the front of the movie theater, I can remember thinking, "God, I wish we were bigger than we are right now." I remember feeling like God had given me this amazing message to share that day, and there would only be 120 people

① yes I've lived there except 3 ten? + OPEN.TO change me! to be able to do this

there to hear it. In that moment, I remember sensing the Holy Spirit say to my heart, "Matt, be all here. Pastor the people who will show up today. Don't preach to all the empty seats. Speak to the ones who have people in them!"

I have heard that statement several times since then. It seems that no matter what stage our church is at in the present, I've always got my eyes on the next one! I wondered at fifty what it would be like to break 100. Then, at 150 I yearned for 200. At 250 I longed for 300. At 350 I couldn't wait to see 400. Just a week after breaking 400, I wrote in my journal, "God, I wonder what 500 feels like." Today, I've got my sights set on a thousand. (Some things never change, I guess.)

In his book *Visioneering,* Andy Stanley describes it as a "tension": a tension of the vision between what is and what could and should be. I think that's accurate. The trick for up-the-middle church leaders is to *be all here* in the moment, and yet not let down our intensity to see our churches grow.

Don't lower your expectations; change them. Be all here, and in the moment. Your church won't always look this way, and someday you'll look back in sheer amazement at how good God was in the moment you're in right now. Don't miss that! Embrace it. It's worth it.

Success Is Consistently Doing the Small Things Right

In attempting to break through the 400 attendance barrier, the biggest lesson we had to learn was in consistently doing the small things right. In fact, I believe if we could have identified this principle earlier, we would have been much more effective at going up-the-middle.

In January of 2006, we blocked out, as a team, an entire morning to zoom out and take a wide lens view of everything Next Level Church had become. Over the course of the morning, we created a report card. Then we began to grade ourselves in what we considered to be the six key areas of our church. We began with the question: *"What are the top six areas in which we must be excellent in order for us to keep people?"* Another way we asked it was, *"What are the six areas that, if we're not excellent, will cause people to leave our church?"* From those questions stemmed the following six areas of our report card:

1. **Worship and Sunday Morning Presentation.** This area encompassed the entire atmosphere of the auditorium environment of our Sunday morning, not the least of which was worship.

2. **Preaching and Teaching / Communication of the Word.** We knew we had to keep the level of excellence high on how we presented the Word of God through relevance, creativity, and humor.

3. **Kids' Ministry.** We knew if the kids weren't excited and growing and begging their parents to come back, we wouldn't keep the parents. If the parents loved it, and the kids hated it, the family wouldn't be coming back.

4. **Youth Ministry.** In order to impact families with teens, we had to have programming for that age group. This was a tough one for us because none of us on the leadership team have kids in that age group, but we knew at that point, it was a priority.

5. **Connection Groups.** As NLC grew bigger, we knew the ability for it to grow smaller at the same time was essential. If we didn't have an environment in our church where people could be known, then we wouldn't impact them.

6. **Pastoral Care.** We came to define pastoral care as making sure people are known, touched, and cared for; however, there is one thing missing from that definition. The final part of the definition involves the perception of availability of our leadership team. If people didn't feel like we were available to them, in their minds, we

weren't. We knew that as our church was growing larger, we still had to be touchable in the people's eyes.

After analyzing our "performance" in these six areas, we then gave ourselves an honest grade. As you can imagine, when you start down this road, it can get really touchy, really quickly. We had to be able to honestly say, "No opinion is off the table." After all, we knew if we wanted to get better as a church at reaching and keeping people, the baseline was honesty, whether it hurt or not.

In addition to giving ourselves a one to ten score in each of the categories, we also assessed the number of paid staff hours we were designating to each of these areas. Our logic was that if these are the six essential keys to keeping people at NLC, then it only makes sense that we should be dedicating as many paid staff hours as possible to them. This is where we began to see the breakdown for us. We became aware that the majority of our paid staff hours were focusing on adult ministry only: connection groups and our Sunday morning auditorium. We had huge holes in our youth, children's ministries, and pastoral care areas. So we put all the job descriptions on the table, and reassigned priorities for each of us.

I can't tell you the impact that meeting had on our church. Several months on the other side of that meeting, we began to see the trust level of our people go sky high. It required big sacrifices and changes on the part of our team, but the end result was that we began consistently doing the small things right, and that paid tremendous dividends in the form of life-change.

I am thoroughly convinced the key for our growing from 300 to 400 was found in this principle of *consistently doing the small things* *right.* Establishing trust in the minds of NLC attendees for an extended period of time made all the difference in the world.

Matt Keller

Success Is Personally Recommitting to the Vision

A friend of mine who had been a veteran of youth ministry for twenty years, once told me how every four years, he would graduate a crop of great students in his youth ministry. He told me that in that time of transition, he would go into a period of real soul-searching that was centered around one question: *Can I do this again?* He would look at the incoming crop of freshmen and think, *"Do I have it in me to develop this group for the next four years?"* He told me he went through this a number of times throughout his tenure in youth ministry.

In January of 2006, we celebrated four years of being in Southwest Florida. I came into that time with mixed emotions, feelings similar to what my friend had felt. In one regard, I was amazed at all God had done. In another regard, I was feeling like the church I was going to be pastoring wasn't the church I had planted four years earlier. Let me explain...

Planting a church requires an entrepreneurial gift. It is impossible to survive a church plant without it. It was the possession of that gift that gave me the courage to move across the country, start with nothing, and just keep pushing it up-the-middle, even when outwardly things looked rough. As we broke into the four year mark of our church, however, I began to realize the church I now pastored wasn't a "start up" anymore. I realized I wasn't a church planter anymore; I was simply a local church pastor. For those of you who have done this, you know what I'm talking about. Suddenly, the excuses were gone. No more, "We're just starting out..." Oh no, you've been going for four years; either you have it together, or you don't.

The dilemma I found myself in was the same as what my youth pastor friend had described years before. I saw my role shifting from church planter and entrepreneur, to pastor, leader, and coach. Over the course of about three weeks, I spent a lot of time praying and

172

connecting with God. It was a good day when I broke through and felt myself "sign on" for another four years!

Redefining my role in our church helped me steer my perspectives and leadership. I prioritize a great deal more of my time to leadership development and releasing. I desire for the team of young leaders around me to flourish even above myself. I see my greatest success as helping them become everything God wants for them to become. Redefining my role caused me to redefine success!

Success is Focusing Individual Priorities

In June of 2006, five months after our initial report card meeting, we took a two-day leadership retreat to Fort Myers Beach. (It's fun to live in a place where we can drive twenty minutes and feel hours from home!) At the retreat, we reviewed the six essential areas of our report card and assigned ourselves a new grade for each area. It was great to monitor the progress we had made in many of the areas. At the end of the two days, I asked each person on our team to answer one question: *In order for Next Level Church to grow like it has the potential to in the next six months, what are the three things that you must do?*

It was amazing to see the light bulbs coming on for each of us. Suddenly, all the busy work of our jobs began to fade to the back as the true priorities of our departments emerged. That one question made it possible for each of us to see what our "must do" list looked like for the next six months. We intend to ask that question of ourselves every six months. With that kind of focus, success is more attainable!

Success is Significance, Even If It's Not Big

We live in a numbers-driven world. The primary determinant of success in our culture almost always looks numerical. In church

CORE TEAM MEETING
"B.O. wins"
LIFE change!

work, however, numbers are one of the worst definitions of success possible. Yet for most of us, it's the one we judge our success by the most. Redefining success is learning to look beyond the numbers to life-change.

Numerical attendance is a poor determinant of success because there are just too many variables involved. Think about the logic for a second. A family decides to get out of town for the weekend last minute... consequently, we're unsuccessful because they didn't show up on Sunday. Someone comes down with the flu and can't make it to church... consequently, we're not successful. Someone sleeps in... we're a failure. Someone goes golfing... we're worthless. Unfortunately, that's how too many of us feel, isn't it? For far too many, personal self-worth and definition of success is directly tied to Sunday morning attendance. The problem with that logic is it's completely arbitrary and unrelated.

Attendance (and offerings) definitely tells a story. But the stories they tell unfold over an extended period of time, not from week to week. To allow our self-worth to get caught up in how many people did or didn't show up last weekend sets us up for failure. We learned that the average church will only ever have about two thirds of its congregation in attendance on any given Sunday. Of course, the obvious exceptions are Christmas and Easter; but on any average weekend, you'll only have about two thirds. That means if your church averages 300 on a Sunday morning, then it's safe to say there are 450 people who call your church their home church. In light of all of this, start re-training yourself to look beyond the numbers. You'll sleep better if you do.

Although we often think significance is found in numbers, we must realized that true significance is found in the individual stories and testimonies of life-change. Never take for granted the stories you hear of how peoples' lives are changed by what you're doing. Cherish them. That is the true definition of our success. Get over it needing to be big. Significance is found in the one, not the many. As pastors, we want this thing to be big; however, if we're ever going to *feel* successful, then we have to get our eyes off of the many and place them on the individual, where they belong.

God has trusted you to love, care for, and pastor the individual people in your church during this season. You have the ability to impart something to them that will change their lives forever. That's a big deal. When we realize that, we're redefining success!

Our prayer as a leadership team over the past several years has been that God would find us trustworthy. God is not going to put in our care more than we can handle. After all, we're not selling widgets, we're impacting people, and people matter to God! In His eyes, this is serious business. Our prayer has been, "God make us trustworthy." When God feels He can trust us, then He'll add to us. Until then, our prayer must be for Him to keep working on us, not just through us. May God make us into the leaders He wants us to be. When we become that, we will have redefined success!

Success Is Life-Change...Period

At the end of the day, it's not about how many people were in the seats, or how big the offering was; it's about the lives that were changed. In redefining success, this one must hit us the hardest. Earlier in the book, I shared the need to celebrate the small victories. When we realize it is about life-change, we suddenly find reason to celebrate, much more often. Never underestimate the lives that are being changed every week.

You have the opportunity to pour into church attendees, small group leaders, children, your spouse, and other peers in ministry. Don't take any of these interactions lightly. You never know when a word in due season, as Proverbs says, will change a life. If you can do that just one time this week, you're a success!

Success Is Being Faithful to Your Journey

More than the numbers or the size of your organization, success is about being faithful, even when it doesn't look like you think it ought to. God has chosen a unique journey for each of us. Mine will not look like yours. Yours will not look like the guy down the road. That's okay. Success isn't based on horizontal comparisons, but on vertical obedience.

I was speaking with a church planter a while back who was struggling with discouragement. His biggest hang up was that his church didn't look like he thought it was going to. In the course of the conversation I shared with him this picture. I said, "You think you're called to paint a specific size of barn in a specific shade of red, but I think that you're just called to paint." Stop worrying about the color or the size of the barn. Let God figure out the details. You just paint.

For too many of us, we have narrowed the possibilities of God by the expectations we have placed on ourselves. We have a picture of what we think God ought to do. When it doesn't look like the picture in our head, we end up missing the very move of God happening right in front of us. By focusing on all that *isn't* happening, we're missing all that *is* happening! We think that because the paint is blue, we're not being successful. What if God thinks we should just shut up and paint? What if we let him worry about the details? What if success is painting where we are? If we're painting to change one life, then we *are* being successful. Don't let anyone tell you any differently, including yourself!

Concluding Thoughts on Redefining Success

At the end of the day, it's not about the speed your church grows, or the amount of people who show up on a Sunday. At the end of the day, it's about being faithful to hear and obey the voice of God in your heart. When I realized that, everything changed. Suddenly the "long-bomb" wasn't necessary anymore. If it happens, great. If it doesn't, then we'll just keep going up-the-middle, and that will be a success!

Chapter 14

Questions for the Huddle

1. How has the reality of your ministry and the expectations you had going in differed? Spend some time as a team discussing how to create accurate expectations for your church going forward.

2. Are you doing the small things right consistently? Spend some time as a team talking about the level of trust that is being created in each of the environments of your church. Discuss all six areas from this chapter.

3. Do you need to recommit to the vision of God for your church? Spend some time as a team encouraging each other and determining how you celebrate the stories of life-change every week in your church.

*Positioning Your Church
for the Long-Bomb*

Up-the-middle churches approach ministry differently

I remember playing backyard football with my brother and our friends growing up. I remember being in the huddle with kids who were older and bigger than I was–kids I admired and feared all at the same time. It seemed every time we huddled up, the backyard quarterback would call the same play: *Go Deep!* He'd point to one guy, "Go deep left." Then to another, "you, go deep right." The rest of us were supposed to block. We didn't win with this strategy too often. It wasn't hard for the defense to figure out, and we were putting a lot of stock in the long-bomb. Looking back now, I realize we would have had a lot more success if we would have ran the ball up-the-middle more often.

The same is true in the church world now. Too many churches are counting on going deep for their entire strategy. Sadly, we're not being effective at putting points on the board in the category of changed lives. Perhaps we need to understand one final principle:

Being faithful to run the ball up-the-middle,

positions us for the long bombs.

As we conclude this book, I want to call the leaders of the up-the-middle church to begin embracing this idea that is both scriptural and powerful. Up-the-middle is the new normal. We will miss long-bomb opportunities if we don't do the hard work of grinding it out, yard by yard, over the long haul.

I know of so many stories of churches who were faithful for several years, even decades before God gave them a long-bomb. Granger Community Church in South Bend, IN is one such story. Mark Beeson and his team had a dream to make an impact for God in their city. It took close to two decades before GCC began to hold any notoriety in the church community.

Seacoast Church in Charleston, SC also has a similar story. My friend Greg Surratt moved to Charleston in the 80's, and for more than a decade, served God in relative obscurity, doing ministry one yard at a time. Today, Seacoast is influencing the church world by leading the way in the multi-site revolution.

And the list goes on and on. The long-bomb churches seem to get all the press, but behind the scenes, there are up-the-middle churches everywhere who are taking ground for God and redefining what the church of tomorrow will look like in every way.

May that be said of each of us as we are faithful to fulfill God's calling and vision for our lives and churches. May we not give up when we get knocked down, fumble the ball, or only pick up a few yards at a time. May we always strive to see that being faithful up-the-middle is what positions us for the long-bomb!

Our Up-the-Middle Journey...

If you would have asked me at the beginning if I wanted an up-the-middle reality for our church, I would have emphatically said no.

But now, I wouldn't change it for any other experience on the planet. Up-the-middle is our journey, and it's the new normal in the church world today.

Thanks for reading,

Matt Keller
Lead Pastor, Next Level Church; Fort Myers, Florida - Est. 2002

For more information & other resources visit...

www.UptheMiddle.com

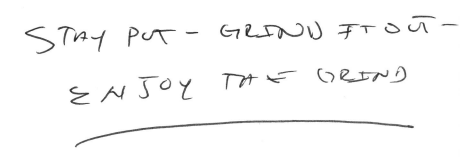

STAY PUT - GRIND IT OUT -
ENJOY THE GRIND

About the ARC

In January of 2003, I had the privilege of connecting with a group of guys who have a passion for planting churches and funding world missions that is unmatched by anything I have ever seen. The Association of Related Churches (ARC) began in 2001 with a vision to start 2000 churches by 2020 and generate $100 Million per year for world missions.

The first two ARC churches began on the same day in February of 2001: New Life Church in Little Rock, AK, pastored by Rick Bezet, and the other, Church of the Highlands in Birmingham, AL, pastored by Chris Hodges. Both churches have grown to several thousand in weekly attendance and serve as a model for churches all across the country and beyond.

The strategy of the ARC for planting life-giving churches is simple, relevant, and relationally driven. Over the past several years, I have been privileged to serve with these guys by offering coaching and support to many of the young churches in the ARC.

Doing church up-the-middle can be lonely. I know that all too well. If you are not connected to a group of people that consistently offers life, encouragement, and support, I hope you will consider the ARC. We would love to have you.

For more information check out:

www.ARCchurches.com

About the Author

Matt Keller is the lead pastor of Next Level Church in Fort Myers, FL. Matt is a passionate communicator who uses humor and story telling to captivate audiences in the weekly services of Next Level Church and across the country. Since its humble beginnings in 2002, Next Level Church has grown from four people to nearly 1,000 attendees in their weekend experiences.

Matt has a heart to help *the little guy* in the church world and frequently travels and consults with pastors of *up-the-middle* churches across the United States. With a heart for church planting, pastoring, leadership development, and consulting, Matt is a leading voice in the next generation of leaders in the church world today.

Matt and his wife, Sarah, have two boys, Will and Drew.

Books Cited

Bedbury, Scott, *A New Brand World*, Penguin Publishers, 2003

Clinton, Robert J., *The Making of a Leader*, NavPress (Colorado Springs, CO), 1988

Collins, Jim, *Good to Great*, Collins Business, 2001

Feldhahn, Shaunti, *For Women Only*, Multnomah Publishers (Sisters, OR) 2004

Feldhahn, Jeff and Shaunti, *For Men Only*, Multnomah Publishers (Sisters, OR), 2006

Gendlin, Eugene, *Experiencing and the Creation of Meaning*, Northwestern University Press, 1997

Godin, Seth, *Purple Cow*, Portfolio Trade, 2003

Hughes, Mark, *Buzzmarketing*, Portfolio Trade, 2008

Kiyosaki, Robert T., *Before You Quit your Job*, Warner Business Books (New York, NY) 2005

Michelli, Joseph A., *The Starbucks Experience*, McGraw-Hill, 2006

Ries, Al, *The Fall of Marketing and the Rise of PR*, Collins Business, 2004

Searcy, Nelson and Kerrick Thomas, *Launch*, Regal Books (Ventura, CA), 2006

Stanley, Andy, *Communicating for a Change*, Multnomah, (Sisters, OR), 2006

Stanley, Andy, *Visioneering*, Multnomah Publishers (Sisters, OR), 2005

Stevens, Mark, *Your Marketing Sucks*, Crown Business, 2003

Churches Cited

Church of the Highlands, Pastor Chris Hodges
(www.ChurchoftheHighlands.com)

Calvary Chapel of New Port Richey, FL, Pastor Bill Strayer
(www.CCWC.org)

Northpoint Community Church, Andy Stanley
(www.NorthPoint.org)

Fellowship Church, Ed Young Jr.
(www.FellowshipChurch.com)

Seacoast Church, Pastor Greg Surratt
(www.Seacoast.org)

Bayside Community Church, Pastor Randy Bezet
(www.BaysideCommunity.org)

Granger Community Church, Pastor Mark Beeson
(www.gccwired.com)

Acknowledgements

To my wife, Sarah: Thanks for having the courage to take this journey with me. The world will never know what we went through in those early days. Thanks for spending your life with me. There's no one else I would rather spend mine with!

To Mike Ash: It hardly seems possible that God has brought us so far. Thanks for being the best right-hand-man I could ever ask for. You're the best friend a guy could want!

To Dave Donahue: You were there in the beginning, man. You are one of only four people who will ever know what that felt like. Dinner every night at the card table in the apartment, dreaming of what church could look like. Only the four of us will ever know what that was like! Thanks for being there.

To the supporters in the early days: You were the ones who believed in this thing when very few others did. You will never know what your financial and prayer support did for us. It truly made all the difference in the world.

To Scott Drummond: I can't even tell you how those phone calls every week kept me sane enough to try again another week. I'm so pumped we get to live this out together now.

To Next Level Church: I love what we've become together. Thanks for making the dream come true!

To my mom and dad: Thanks for letting us live in the house for the first five and a half years of this thing. You guys subsidized our life in so many ways. This book and all that I do for others is my way of paying you back.

To Belinda Dufrene: Thanks for running details on this book like a mad woman. You and I both know it would have never gotten done otherwise! You pushed me and here it is!

To Kristin Corder, my editor: Thanks for making this book way better than it was. I can talk, but you helped me write. Thanks.

To Pete and Dr. Julie: Thanks for believing in the vision and getting behind this project. You made this possible!

To John Bolin: Thanks for being a big brother to me in this whole writing process and telling me to *write something everyday!* It worked!

To Billy Hornsby: Thanks for believing in us when we felt like no one else did. Thanks for flying to Florida and eating breakfast with us. Thanks for giving me a platform to impact so many other guys who need encouragement. I am an adopted son!

Finally, to Jesus: It's just abundantly clear, the further we go, that it's all You. It's always been all You, and it always will be all You! Thanks for allowing me to be apart of *Your* dream for *my* life.

Printed in the United States
154737LV00001B/78/P